A Day In BARCELONA, SPAIN
Family Mini Adventure Planner

Family Trip Planner to Barcelona

Trip Planners to Major Cities Across the World, Volume 1

Christopher Neil

Published by Christopher Neil, 2024.

FAMILY TRIP PLANNER TO BARCELONA

First edition. October 20, 2024.

ISBN: 979-8227826664

Written by Christopher Neil.

Table of Contents

Christopher Neil

Dedicated To:

"The world is full of wonderful things you haven't seen yet. Don't ever give up on the chance of seeing them.

"We live in a wonderful world that is full of beauty, charm, and adventure.

There is no end to the adventures we can have if only we seek them with our eyes open."

Quotes

""Barcelona is a fountain of courtesy, shelter of strangers, hospital of the poor, land of the valiant, avenger of the offended, reciprocator of firm friendship, a city unique in its location and beauty." -

MIGUEL DE CERVATES

-

""In Barcelona, I landed in a city with wide boulevards, markets, cafes, kiosks, paseos, beaches, statues, fountains, poets, heroes, modernista lampposts, art nouveau facades: a city built for human beings."

COLM TOIBIN

Contents

Introduction: Welcome to Barcelona! Dear Adventurous Families,

¡Bienvenidos a Barcelona! Welcome to the vibrant, sun-soaked jewel of Catalonia! We're thrilled that you've chosen to explore this magical city with your loved ones. Barcelona is a place where ancient history dances with cutting-edge modernity, where the Mediterranean Sea whispers tales of explorers past, and where every street corner holds the promise of a new discovery.

Imagine strolling down Las Ramblas, the city's famous promenade, hand-in-hand with your little ones as street performers entertain with dazzling acts. Picture your family gazing in awe at the whimsical creations of Antoni Gaudí, from the fairy-tale spires of the Sagrada Família to the colorful mosaics of Park Güell. Can you hear the excited chatter of your children as they spot the dragons and gargoyles adorning the city's unique architecture?

Barcelona is a city that speaks to the child in all of us. It's a place where imagination runs wild, where history comes alive, and where the spirit of adventure is as palpable as the aroma of freshly baked bread wafting from the local panaderías. Whether you're exploring the narrow, winding streets of the Gothic Quarter, cheering for FC Barcelona at Camp Nou, or building sandcastles on Barceloneta Beach, this city offers a treasure trove of experiences for families of all ages.

So, pack your sense of wonder, bring your appetite for both food and adventure, and get ready to create memories that will last a lifetime.

Barcelona isn't just a destination; it's an experience that will captivate hearts young and old. Let's embark on this journey together!

How to Use This Book

Welcome to your family's personal guide to Barcelona! We've designed this book to be your trusty companion as you navigate the enchanting streets and hidden gems of this remarkable city. Here's how to make the most of your Mini-Adventure Planner:

1. **Choose Your Own Adventure**: Each chapter in this book represents a different themed adventure. You can tackle them in any order you like, based on your family's interests and energy levels.

2. **Age-Appropriate Activities**: Look for the age icons next to each activity:

   - Suitable for ages 3-G
   - Perfect for ages 7-11
   - Engaging for ages 12-15

   But remember, these are just suggestions. You know your children best!

3. **Time Management**: We've included estimated durations for each activity. Use these as a guide to plan your day, but feel free to linger where you're having fun!

   4. **Interactive Elements**: Keep an eye out for:
   - Fun Facts: Interesting tidbits to share with your kids
   - Tips: Helpful advice to make your adventure smoother
   - Activity Boxes: Hands-on tasks to keep little hands busy

   5. **Flexibility is Key**: Remember, this is your adventure. Feel free to mix and match activities or even create your own based on our suggestions.

> **Family Adventure Anecdote**: The García family from Mexico City used this guide last summer. Nine-year-old Sofia says, "I loved how we could choose what to do each day. One morning we were pirates in the maritime museum, and in the afternoon, we were architects designing our own Gaudí-inspired buildings!"

G. **Local Lingo**: We've sprinkled some Catalan and Spanish phrases throughout the book. Try them out – locals appreciate the effort!

7. **Rainy Day Plans**: Look for the ☂ symbol for indoor activity alternatives.

8. **Family Challenges**: Each chapter includes a fun family challenge. Complete them all to earn the title of "Barcelona Adventure Champions"!

Remember, the best adventures are the ones where everyone has fun. So, take breaks when needed, always have snacks on hand, and don't forget to enjoy the journey as much as the destination!

About the City

Barcelona, the capital of Catalonia, is a city that seamlessly blends the old with the new, the traditional with the avant-garde. With a history spanning over 2,000 years, this Mediterranean metropolis has been shaped by Romans, Visigoths, Moors, and Catalans, each leaving their unique mark on its culture and landscape.

Founded as the Roman colony of Barcino in the 1st century BC, Barcelona's ancient roots are still visible in the ruins scattered throughout the city. As you walk through the Gothic Quarter, you'll be treading on stones that have witnessed centuries of history. Imagine the stories these walls could tell!

◇ **Fun Fact**: Did you know that Barcelona has a subterranean Roman city? Parts of it can be seen in the Barcelona City History Museum!

Fast forward to the Middle Ages, and Barcelona had become a major maritime power, evident in the grand Gothic structures like the Cathedral of the Holy Cross and Saint Eulalia. The city's golden age in the 14th and 15th centuries left behind architectural marvels that your family will explore, from the imposing city walls to the charming squares of the old town.

But it's the late 19th and early 20th centuries that truly defined Barcelona's unique character. This was the era of Modernisme, the Catalan version of Art Nouveau, which gave birth to some of the city's most iconic landmarks. The genius of architects like Antoni Gaudí transformed Barcelona into an open-air museum of whimsical, nature-inspired buildings that seem to have sprung from a fairy tale.

Tip: Challenge your kids to spot animal and plant shapes in Gaudí's buildings. It's a great way to keep them engaged during sightseeing!

Today, Barcelona is a bustling metropolis of 1.G million people (5.5 million in the greater urban area), known for its vibrant arts scene, cutting-edge cuisine, and passion for sports. It's a city where you can start your day admiring Picasso's early works, spend the afternoon on a sunny beach, and end the evening cheering for Barça at a football match.

The city's layout is a testament to its evolution. The narrow, labyrinthine streets of the old town open up to the wide, tree-lined avenues of the 19th-century Eixample district. Each neighborhood has its own distinct flavor:

- **Barri Gòtic**: The heart of old Barcelona, with its medieval alleyways and hidden plazas.

- **El Born**: A trendy area filled with boutique shops, cafes, and the stunning Santa Maria del Mar church.

- **Eixample**: Home to the majority of Modernista architecture and upscale shopping.

- **Gràcia**: A bohemian district with a village-like feel, popular with young families.

- **Barceloneta**: The city's most famous beach neighborhood, perfect for soaking up the Mediterranean vibe.

Barcelona's Mediterranean climate means you can enjoy outdoor activities almost year-round. Summers are warm and perfect for beach days, while winters are mild and ideal for exploring the city's many parks and gardens.

5

The city's cuisine is a reflection of its coastal location and rich cultural heritage. From traditional Catalan dishes like pa amb tomàquet (bread with tomato) and fideuà (a paella-like dish made with noodles) to innovative tapas creations, Barcelona is a food lover's paradise. And don't worry, even the pickiest eaters in your family will find something to love!

Activity Box: Draw your dream Gaudí-inspired building! What shapes and colors would you use?

Barcelona is also a city of festivals and traditions. If you're lucky, you might catch the colorful Festes de Gràcia in August, where entire streets are transformed into fantastical themed displays. Or perhaps you'll witness the human towers (castells) being built during La Mercè festival in September – a breathtaking sight that showcases the Catalan spirit of teamwork and daring.

As you explore Barcelona, you'll notice that it's a bilingual city. Both Catalan and Spanish are official languages, and you'll hear both spoken on the streets. Don't be surprised to see signs in both languages – it's part of the city's unique identity.

Fun Fact: Barcelona is home to 9 UNESCO World Heritage Sites, 7 of which were designed by Antoni Gaudí!

From its sun-drenched beaches to its mystical mountains, from its gothic spires to its modernist marvels, Barcelona is a city that captivates all who visit. It's a place where history is alive, where creativity flourishes, and where every street corner holds the potential for a new family adventure.

Additional Information

As you prepare for your Barcelona adventure, here are some extra tidbits to get your family excited and ready for the journey ahead:

Barcelona for Young Imaginations

Barcelona is a city that seems to have sprung from the pages of a storybook, making it perfect for nurturing young imaginations. Encourage your children to let their creativity soar:

- **Dragon Hunt**: Barcelona is full of dragon imagery. Challenge your kids to spot as many dragons as they can throughout the city. They're on buildings, in parks, and even on street furniture!

- **Fairy Tale Architecture**: Gaudí's buildings look like they're straight out of a fairy tale. Ask your children what kind of stories they think could happen in these magical places.

- **Beach Sculpture Competition**: On Barceloneta Beach, have a family competition to see who can create the most imaginative sand sculpture inspired by what you've seen in the city.

1. Barcelona for Young Imaginations

Barcelona is a city that seems to have sprung from the pages of a storybook, making it perfect for nurturing young imaginations. Encourage your children to let their creativity soar:

- **Dragon Hunt**: Barcelona is full of dragon imagery. Challenge your kids to spot as many dragons as they can throughout the city. They're on buildings, in parks, and even on street furniture!

- **Fairy Tale Architecture**: Gaudí's buildings look like they're straight out of a fairy tale. Ask your children what kind of stories they think could happen in these magical places.

- **Beach Sculpture Competition**: On Barceloneta Beach, have a family competition to see who can create the most imaginative sand sculpture inspired by what you've seen in the city.

2. Green Spaces and Outdoor Adventures

While Barcelona is known for its urban charm, it also offers plenty of green spaces for kids to run, play, and explore:

- **Park Güell**: Beyond Gaudí's famous architectural elements, there are woodland paths to explore and stunning city views to enjoy.

- **Montjuïc**: This hill overlooking the city is home to several parks, gardens, and even an old castle to explore.

- **Parc de la Ciutadella**: Barcelona's central park is perfect for picnics, rowing boats, and visiting the small zoo.

- **Tibidabo**: This mountain offers hiking trails and an amusement park with spectacular views over Barcelona.

Tip: Many of Barcelona's parks have excellent playgrounds. They're perfect for letting the kids burn off some energy while you take a short break!

3. Family-Friendly Museums

Barcelona's museums aren't just for adults. Many offer interactive exhibits and programs designed specifically for children:
    - **CosmoCaixa**: This science museum is a hit with kids of all ages, featuring a planetarium and a flooded Amazon rainforest exhibit.
    - **Barcelona Maritime Museum**: Housed in medieval shipyards, this museum lets kids explore life at sea through the ages.
    - **Chocolate Museum**: Learn about the history of chocolate and admire sculptures made entirely of chocolate!
    - **FC Barcelona Museum**: For young football fans, this is a must-visit to learn about one of the world's most famous clubs.

.4. Getting Around with Kids

Barcelona has an excellent public transportation system that's easy to navigate with children:

    - The metro and bus network covers most of the city.

    - Trams and funiculars can be a fun transportation experience in themselves.
    - Many of the city's main attractions are within walking distance of each other, especially in the old town.
    Tip: Consider getting a Hola Barcelona Travel Card for unlimited trips on public transport. Kids under 4 travel free!

5. Family-Friendly Festivals

If your visit coincides with one of Barcelona's many festivals, you're in for a treat:

- **La Mercè** (September): The city's biggest street party features giants, dragons, and human tower competitions.

- **Sant Jordi** (April 23): Barcelona's version of Valentine's Day, where books and roses are exchanged. The streets fill with book and flower stalls.

- **Festes de Gràcia** (August): A week-long street decoration competition and festival in the Gràcia neighborhood.

G. Beach Time

Don't forget that Barcelona is a beach city! With 4.5km of sandy shores, there's plenty of space for family fun:

- Barceloneta is the most famous beach, but families might prefer the quieter Bogatell or Mar Bella beaches.

- Many beaches have play areas, volleyball courts, and chiringuitos (beach bars) for snacks and drinks.

Fun Fact: The city's beaches are man-made, created for the 1992 Olympics!

7. Family-Friendly Dining

Catalan cuisine is delicious, but we know kids can sometimes be picky eaters. Here are some tips:
- Many restaurants offer "menú del día" - a fixed price menu that often includes child-friendly options.
- Try introducing your kids to tapas - the small portions are perfect for trying new things.
- Look for family-friendly restaurants with play areas, especially common in the Gràcia and Poblenou neighborhoods.
- Don't miss trying Spanish omelette (tortilla), croquettes, and of course, paella!
. 8. Learning Opportunities
Turn your family trip into an educational adventure:
- Encourage older kids to learn a few phrases in Catalan or Spanish before the trip.
- Discuss the unique Catalan culture and how it differs from other parts of Spain.
- Use Gaudí's architecture to introduce concepts of biology, geometry, and engineering.

- Explore the city's Roman and medieval history in the Gothic Quarter.

11

9. Rainy Day Plans

While Barcelona enjoys a lot of sunshine, it's good to have some indoor options:

- **L'Aquàrium**: One of Europe's largest aquariums, great for a rainy afternoon.

- **Poble Espanyol**: An open-air museum showcasing architecture from around Spain, with many indoor craft workshops.

- **Casa Batlló** or **La Pedrera**: Gaudí's indoor marvels are perfect for escaping bad weather.

10. Safety and Comfort

A few final tips to ensure your family's comfort and safety:

- Barcelona is generally very safe, but like any big city, be aware of pickpockets in tourist areas.

- Summers can be hot - remember hats, sunscreen, and stay hydrated.
- Many shops close for a siesta in the afternoon - plan accordingly.

- Dinner time in Barcelona is typically later than in many countries - around 9 pm. Plan for late lunches or early dinners with kids.

few final tips to ensure your family's comfort and safety:

- Barcelona is generally very safe, but like any big city, be aware of pickpockets in tourist areas.

- Summers can be hot - remember hats, sunscreen, and stay hydrated.
- Many shops close for a siesta in the afternoon - plan accordingly.

- Dinner time in Barcelona is typically later than in many countries - around 9 pm. Plan for late lunches or early dinners with kids.

10

With all this in mind, you're ready to embark on your Barcelona adventure! Remember, the key to a great family trip is flexibility, a sense of humor, and a willingness to embrace new experiences. Barcelona is a city that rewards curiosity, so encourage your children to ask questions, try new things, and immerse themselves in the vibrant Catalan culture.

From the sun-drenched beaches to the whimsical architecture, from the bustling markets to the peaceful parks, Barcelona offers a world of discovery for families. Every corner of this enchanting city holds the potential for a new adventure, a learning opportunity, or a moment of wonder.

So pack your sunscreen, charge your camera, and get ready to make memories that will last a lifetime. Your Barcelona adventure awaits!

¡Que os divirtáis! Have fun!

1

CHAPTER ONE - Planning Your Adventure in Barcelona

Welcome, adventurous families! You're about to embark on an unforgettable journey to the vibrant city of Barcelona. This guide will help you prepare for your trip, navigate the city with ease, stay safe, and get excited about all the amazing experiences awaiting you in the Catalan capital.

Preparing for Your Trip Packing Essentials

Before you set off on your Barcelona adventure, make sure you've got all the essentials packed. Here's a handy checklist to get you started:

- [ ] Comfortable walking shoes (you'll be doing lots of exploring!)
- [ ] Light, breathable clothing for warm days
- [ ] Light jacket or sweater for cooler evenings
- [ ] Sunscreen, sunglasses, and hats for sun protection
- [ ] Reusable water bottles for the whole family
- [ ] Backpack or day bag for carrying essentials during outings
- [ ] Camera or smartphone for capturing memories
- [ ] Power bank and adapters (Spain uses Type C and F plugs)
- [ ] Basic first aid kit
- [ ] Hand sanitizer and wet wipes
- [ ] Snacks for hungry little explorers

Tip for Parents: Pack a few small, familiar toys or games for younger children. They can be a lifesaver during downtime or when waiting in lines!

Documents and Bookings

Ensure you have all necessary documents and bookings in order:

- Valid passports for all family members
- Travel insurance documents
- Copies of important documents (store separately from originals)
- Hotel or accommodation bookings
- Flight tickets or boarding passes
- Any pre-booked attraction tickets or passes

Language Basics

While many people in Barcelona speak English, learning a few basic phrases in Spanish (and Catalan, if you're feeling adventurous!) can go a long way. Here are some useful phrases to practice with your kids:

English	Spanish	Catalan
————-	————-	—
Hello	Hola	Hola
Thank you	Gracias	Gràcies
Please	Por favor	Si us plau
Excuse me	Perdón	Perdó
Where is...?	¿Dónde está...?	On és ?
Goodbye	Adiós	Adéu

Make it a fun family activity to practice these phrases before your trip!

1

Weather Watch

Barcelona enjoys a Mediterranean climate with mild winters and warm summers. However, it's always a good idea to check the forecast before you pack. Here's a general guide:

  - **Spring (March-May)**: Mild temperatures, occasional rain. Pack layers and a light raincoat.

  - **Summer (June-August)**: Hot and sunny. Don't forget swimwear for beach days!

  - **Fall (September-November)**: Warm days, cooler nights. Bring a mix of light and warmer clothing.

  - **Winter (December-February)**: Cool but rarely freezing. Pack warm layers and a waterproof jacket.

  Fun Fact: Barcelona averages 2,524 hours of sunshine per year! That's a lot of sunny days for outdoor adventures.

Tech Prep

In today's digital age, a little tech prep can make your trip much smoother:

1. Download offline maps of Barcelona to your smartphone.
2. Install translation apps like Google Translate or iTranslate.
3. Consider getting a local SIM card or an international data plan for easy internet access.
4. Download entertainment apps or e-books for the kids to enjoy during downtime.

Public Transportation

Barcelona's public transportation network is extensive and includes metros, buses, trams, and trains.

Involve the Kids

Get your children excited about the trip by involving them in the planning process:

- Have them research fun facts about Barcelona and share with the family.

- Let older kids help plan the itinerary by choosing activities they're interested in.

- Create a countdown calendar to build anticipation.
- Encourage them to start a travel journal or scrapbook.

Family Activity Idea: Host a Spanish-themed dinner night at home before your trip. Try making paella or tapas, play Spanish music, and practice your language skills!

Navigating the City

Barcelona is a large city, but with its efficient public transportation system and pedestrian-friendly areas, getting around is a breeze. Here's what you need to know:

Navigating the City

Barcelona is a large city, but with its efficient public transportation system and pedestrian-friendly areas, getting around is a breeze. Here's what you need to know:

17

Public Transportation

Barcelona's public transportation network is extensive and includes metros, buses, trams, and trains.

Metro

The metro is fast, efficient, and covers most of the city. It's an excellent option for families:

- **Hours**: Mon-Thu, Sun and holidays: 5:00 AM - 12:00 AM; Fri and evenings before holidays: 5:00 AM - 2:00 AM; Sat: Non-stop service

"*Tickets**: Various options available, including single tickets, multi-day passes, and the Hola Barcelona Travel Card

- **Family-Friendly Features**: Elevators at most stations, wide carriages for strollers

Tip: The Hola Barcelona Travel Card offers unlimited trips on public transport and includes airport transfers. It's a great option for families planning to use public transport frequently.

Buses

Buses complement the metro system and can be a good option for reaching areas not covered by the metro:

- **Hours**: Vary by route, but many run from 4:25 AM to 11:00 PM

- **Night Buses**: Available from 11:00 PM to G:00 AM

- **Features**: Most buses are wheelchair and stroller accessible

_-*

Trams

A Day In BARCELONA , SPAIN
19

Trams operate in the outer areas of the city and can be a fun ride for kids:

- **Routes**: Six lines (T1-TG) serving the outskirts of Barcelona
- **Hours**: Generally from 5:00 AM to 12:00 AM (may vary by line)

Walking

Barcelona is a very walkable city, especially in the central areas:
- Many attractions are within walking distance of each other in the Gothic Quarter and El Born.
- Walking allows you to discover hidden gems and enjoy the city's beautiful architecture.
- Consider taking walking breaks for younger children to explore playgrounds or parks along your route.

Taxes and Ride-sharing

Taxis are readily available and can be a convenient option for families with young children:

- Official Barcelona taxis are black and yellow.

- Most taxis can accommodate child seats, but it's best to request one in advance.

- Ride-sharing apps like Cabify are also available in Barcelona.

Bicycle and Scooter Rentals

For families with older children, renting bicycles or scooters can be a fun way to explore:

- Many rental shops offer child seats, trailers, or smaller bikes for kids.

- Barcelona has an extensive network of bike lanes, making cycling safer and easier.

- Always wear helmets and follow traffic rules.

Safety Tip: If cycling, stick to dedicated bike lanes and less crowded streets. Avoid busy areas like Las Ramblas on a bike.

Navigating with Kids

- **Stroller-Friendly Routes**: Many areas in Barcelona are stroller-friendly, but some older parts of the city have narrow or cobblestone streets.
Consider bringing a lightweight, sturdy stroller.
- **Rest Stops**: Plan your routes with potential rest stops in mind. Parks, cafes, and attractions where kids can take a break are plentiful throughout the city.
- **Meeting Points**: Establish meeting points in case anyone gets separated, especially in crowded areas like La Boqueria market or Parc Güell.
> **Family Challenge**: Turn navigation into a game! Let older kids lead the way using a map for short distances, or play "I Spy" with landmarks to keep younger ones engaged during walks.

Safety Tips for Families

Barcelona is generally a safe city for families, but as with any travel destination, it's important to stay aware and take precautions. Here are some tips to ensure your family's safety during your adventure:

Street Smarts

1. **Stay Alert**: Barcelona is known for pickpockets, especially in tourist areas. Keep an eye on your belongings at all times.
    2. **Secure Your Valuables**: Use anti-theft bags or keep valuables in front pockets or hidden pouches.
    3. **Crowd Caution**: Be extra vigilant in crowded areas like Las Ramblas, metro stations, and popular attractions.
    4. **Stranger Danger**: Remind children not to talk to strangers or accept anything from them.

Beach Safety

Barcelona's beaches are beautiful, but require some safety measures:

- Always supervise children near the water.
- Pay attention to beach flags indicating water conditions.
- Apply sunscreen regularly and stay hydrated.
- Be aware of the location of lifeguard stations.

2

Food and Water Safety

While tap water in Barcelona is safe to drink, some may prefer bottled water:

- Stick to bottled water if you're concerned.

- Be cautious with street food, especially for young children.

- Inform restaurants of any food allergies – "Tengo una alergia a..." (I have an allergy to...)

Health Precautions

- Carry a basic first aid kit for minor injuries or illnesses.

- Know the location of the nearest pharmacy (farmacia) to your accommodation.

- Familiarize yourself with emergency numbers:

- General Emergency: 112

- Police: 092

- Ambulance: 0G1 Transportation Safety

- Always use marked pedestrian crossings and obey traffic signals.

- Hold hands with younger children when crossing streets or in busy areas.

- If using public transportation, keep children close and be aware of closing doors.

Transportation Safety

- Always use marked pedestrian crossings and obey traffic signals.

- Hold hands with younger children when crossing streets or in busy areas.

- If using public transportation, keep children close and be aware of closing doors.

22

Sun Protection

Barcelona's sunny climate requires good sun protection:

- Apply high SPF sunscreen regularly.
- Wear hats and sunglasses.
- Seek shade during the hottest parts of the day (usually 12 PM - 3 PM).

Accommodation Safety

- Familiarize your family with emergency exits in your hotel or apartment.
- Set a meeting point outside the accommodation in case of an emergency.
- Use the room safe for passports and valuables.

Family Safety Game: Play the "Buddy System" game where each family member is paired with a "buddy" they need to keep an eye on during outings.

Cultural Sensitivity

Respecting local customs can help avoid uncomfortable situations:

- Dress modestly when visiting religious sites.

- Be mindful of siesta time (usually 2 PM - 4 PM) when some shops may be closed.

- Learn and use basic pleasantries in Spanish or Catalan. Emergency Preparedness

- Save emergency contacts in everyone's phones.

- Write down important information (hotel address, emergency numbers) on a card for each family member to carry.

2

Cultural Sensitivity

Respecting local customs can help avoid uncomfortable situations:

- Dress modestly when visiting religious sites.

- Be mindful of siesta time (usually 2 PM - 4 PM) when some shops may be closed.

- Learn and use basic pleasantries in Spanish or Catalan.

Emergency Preparedness

- Save emergency contacts in everyone's phones.

- Write down important information (hotel address, emergency numbers) on a card for each family member to carry.

- Consider travel insurance for peace of mind.

Teaching Moment: Use your trip as an opportunity to teach kids about travel safety in a positive, non-scary way. Encourage them to be observant and trust their instincts.

Getting Excited for Your Barcelona Adventure

Now that we've covered the practicalities, let's get your family excited about all the amazing experiences awaiting you in Barcelona!

24

Countdown to Adventure
Create a fun countdown to your trip:

- Make a paper chain, removing one link each day.
- Have a daily "Fun Fact about Barcelona" at dinner.

- Learn a new Spanish or Catalan word each day. Virtual Exploration
Before you go, explore Barcelona virtually:

- Take virtual tours of famous sites like Sagrada Familia or Park Güell.
- Watch family-friendly travel vlogs about Barcelona.

- Use Google Street View to "walk" around neighborhoods you plan to visit. Tasty Preparations
Get your taste buds ready for Catalan cuisine:
- Try making simple Spanish dishes at home like tortilla española or pan con tomate.

- Have a family tapas night, sampling small bites of different foods.

- Introduce kids to new flavors they might encounter, like olive oil, manchego cheese, or jamón.
Artistic Inspirations
Barcelona is an art lover's paradise. Introduce your kids to some of the city's famous artists:

25

- Look at pictures of Gaudí's whimsical architecture.
- Try creating Miró-inspired abstract art.

- Watch the movie "Vicky Cristina Barcelona" (for families with older teens) to see the city on screen.
Language Learning Fun
Make learning basic Spanish or Catalan phrases a family activity:

  - Use language learning apps like Duolingo together.
  - Play simple word games or have "Spanish-only" hours at home.

- Watch children's shows in Spanish with subtitles. Pack with Purpose
Get kids involved in packing their own day bags:

  - Let them choose a special notebook or sketchbook for their travel journal.

  - Help them pack a "surprise bag" with small activities for the journey.

- Encourage older kids to research and make a list of things they want to bring.
Dream Itinerary
Have a family brainstorming session about what everyone wants to do in Barcelona:

  - Create a wish list of sights, activities, and foods to try.
  - Look at pictures of different attractions and vote on favorites.
  - Discuss any concerns or questions about the trip openly.

Tip: Remember to balance your itinerary with down time. Even the most exciting trip needs some relaxation!

Capture the Anticipation

Start your travel memories before you even leave:

- Take a "pre-trip" family photo with your packed bags.

- Record a video of everyone sharing what they're most excited about.

- Start a trip hashtag for social media posts (if your family uses social media)

27

Family Bonding Idea: Host a "Barcelona Night" at home. Decorate with Spanish flags, play Catalan music, eat Spanish-inspired food, and share all the exciting plans for your upcoming adventure!

Remember, the joy of travel begins long before you reach your destination. By involving the whole family in the planning and preparation, you're already creating wonderful memories. Barcelona is a city that captivates visitors of all ages with its unique blend of history, culture, and modern vibrancy. From the magical architecture of Gaudí to the bustling energy of La Boqueria market, from the sun-soaked beaches to the winding streets of the Gothic Quarter, your family is in for an unforgettable adventure.

So pack your bags, brush up on your "hola"s and "gracias"s, and get ready to make amazing memories in beautiful Barcelona. Your adventure awaits!

¡Buen viaje! (Have a good trip!)

CHAPTER TWO - Adventure Styles
Overview

Welcome, adventurous families! Barcelona is a treasure trove of experiences waiting to be discovered. Whether you're traveling with toddlers, tweens, or teens, this vibrant city has something for everyone. In this section, we'll explore six unique adventure styles to help you tailor your Barcelona experience to your family's interests and energy levels. Remember, there's no one-size-fits-all approach to family travel – the key is finding the perfect blend of activities that will create lasting memories for your entire crew.

Choosing Your Adventure Style

1. Cultural Explorers

For families who love to immerse themselves in the rich tapestry of local history, art, and traditions, the Cultural Explorers style is perfect.

Barcelona's unique blend of Catalan and Spanish culture offers a wealth of opportunities to engage with the city's heritage.

Highlights:

- Gaudi's architectural wonders (Sagrada Familia, Park Güell, Casa Batlló)
- Museums galore (MNAC, Picasso Museum, CosmoCaixa)
- Traditional festivals and events

Best for:

- Families with curious minds
- Art and history enthusiasts
- Those who enjoy guided tours and interactive exhibits

Kid-Friendly Tip: Many museums offer special family programs or interactive areas designed for younger visitors. Look for hands-on workshops or child-oriented audio guides to keep the little ones engaged.

29

2. Nature Lovers

Barcelona might be known for its urban charm, but it's also a gateway to natural wonders. The Nature Lovers style is perfect for families who crave fresh air, green spaces, and outdoor adventures.
Highlights:

- Collserola Natural Park
- Montjuïc's gardens and cable car
- Barceloneta Beach and water activities

Best for:

- Active families
- Outdoor enthusiasts
- Those seeking a break from city life

Kid-Friendly Tip: Pack a picnic and spend a day exploring Collserola Natural Park. The park offers easy hiking trails suitable for all ages and a chance to spot local wildlife.

3. Foodie Fanatics

Barcelona is a culinary paradise, and the Foodie Fanatics style is perfect for families who bond over delicious meals and new flavors. From traditional Catalan dishes to innovative fusion cuisine, there's something to satisfy every palate.

Highlights:

  - La Boqueria food market
  - Cooking classes for families
  - Tapas tours and chocolate workshops

*Best for:**

  - Adventurous eaters
  - Families who enjoy cooking together
  - Those interested in local culinary traditions

Kid-Friendly Tip: Many cooking classes are designed with families in mind. Look for ones that allow children to participate in preparing simple dishes or desserts.

4. Urban Adventurers

For families who thrive on the energy of city life, the Urban Adventurers style offers a mix of modern attractions and hidden gems off the beaten path.
Highlights:

   - Exploring neighborhoods like Gràcia and El Born
   - Street art tours
   - Unique transportation experiences (e.g., bike tours, funiculars)

Best for:

   - Families who enjoy walking and exploring
   - Those interested in modern culture and lifestyle
   - Adventure-seekers looking for unique urban experiences

Kid-Friendly Tip: Consider a family-friendly bike tour to cover more ground and see the city from a different perspective. Many tour companies offer child seats or tandem bikes for younger children.

5. Beach Bums

With its stunning coastline, Barcelona is perfect for families who love sun, sand, and sea. The Beach Bums style focuses on relaxation and water-based activities.
Highlights:

   - Barceloneta, Mar Bella, and Bogatell beaches
   - Water sports (paddleboarding, kayaking)
   - Beachside playgrounds and activities

Best for:

- Families seeking relaxation
- Water sports enthusiasts
- Those who enjoy combining city and beach vacations

Kid-Friendly Tip: Look for beaches with Blue Flag certification, which ensures clean water and good facilities. Barceloneta Beach often has volleyball nets set up, perfect for family games.

G. Thrill Seekers

For families who crave excitement and adrenaline rushes, the Thrill Seekers style offers a range of heart-pumping activities in and around Barcelona.

Highlights:

- PortAventura World theme park
- Tibidabo Amusement Park
- Indoor skydiving at Windoor

Best for:

- Adventure-loving families
- Older children and teens
- Those looking for unique, high-energy experiences

Kid-Friendly Tip: Tibidabo Amusement Park offers a mix of old-school charm and modern thrills, with rides suitable for various age groups. The views of Barcelona from the top are spectacular!

33

Customizing Your Itinerary

Now that you're familiar with the different adventure styles, it's time to create your perfect Barcelona itinerary. Here are some tips to help you mix and match activities to suit your family's preferences:

1. Balance is Key

While it's tempting to pack your days full of activities, remember that downtime is crucial, especially when traveling with children. Here's a suggested daily structure:

- Morning: Start with a high-energy activity when everyone is fresh
- Afternoon: Mix in some relaxation or free exploration time
- Evening: End with a fun family dinner or a leisurely stroll

2. Mix and Match Adventure Styles

Don't feel confined to just one adventure style. The beauty of Barcelona is its diversity. Try this approach:

1. Choose a primary adventure style that aligns with your family's main interests

2. Sprinkle in activities from other styles to add variety

3. Be flexible and willing to adjust based on your family's mood and energy levels

Example Mix:

- Morning: Visit Park Güell (Cultural Explorers)
- Afternoon: Beach time at Barceloneta (Beach Bums)
- Evening: Tapas tour in El Born (Foodie Fanatics)

3. Consider Your Children's Ages

Different activities appeal to different age groups. Here's a quick guide: Age Group | Recommended Activities |
3-5 years | - Puppet shows at Parc de la Ciutadella
- Aquarium Barcelona
- Magic Fountain of Montjuïc |
G-10 years | - CosmoCaixa Science Museum
- Chocolate Museum workshop
- Park Güell scavenger hunt |
11-15 years | - Bike tour of the city
- Cooking class
- Camp Nou (FC Barcelona stadium) tour |

4. Use Transportation as Part of the Adventure

Barcelona's public transportation system can be an adventure in itself. Consider these options:

- Take the funicular to Montjuïc for stunning views
- Ride the historic Tramvia Blau (Blue Tram) to Tibidabo
- Use the hop-on-hop-off bus to get an overview of the city

5. Plan for Flexibility

Always have a backup plan in case of unexpected weather or closed attractions. Here are some ideas:
Rainy Day Alternatives:

- Indoor playgrounds like Kidszania
- Cinema screenings (look for English-language options)
- Museu de la Xocolata (Chocolate Museum)

3

Too Hot? Try These:

- L'Aquàrium de Barcelona
- Ice Bar experience
- Indoor rock climbing at Sharma Climbing

G. Involve the Whole Family in Planning

Get your children excited about the trip by involving them in the planning process:

1. Present simplified versions of each adventure style
2. Let each family member choose one must-do activity
3. Use a visual planner (like a large calendar or whiteboard) to map out your itinerary

7. Local Insights

Don't be afraid to ask locals or your accommodation staff for recommendations. They often know the best family-friendly spots that might not be in guidebooks.

Tip: Look for "Family-Friendly Barcelona" groups on social media platforms for up-to-date recommendations from other traveling families.

8. Time Management

Barcelona is a large city, and travel times between attractions can add up. Use these strategies to maximize your time:

1. Group activities by neighborhood
2. Use siesta time (2-5 PM) for relaxation or pool time if your accommodation has one
3. Book skip-the-line tickets for popular attractions like Sagrada Familia

9. Embrace Spontaneity

While planning is important, some of the best family memories come from unexpected discoveries. Leave room in your itinerary for:

- Stumbling upon local festivals or street performances
- Exploring charming side streets
- Trying out that quirky-looking café or ice cream shop

10. Capture the Memories

Encourage your children to document the trip in their own way:

- Provide disposable cameras or let them use a phone camera
- Give them a travel journal to write or draw in each day
- Collect small mementos like ticket stubs or postcards for a scrapbook

Remember, the goal is to create a Barcelona adventure that's uniquely tailored to your family. By mixing different adventure styles and remaining flexible, you'll create an itinerary that offers something for everyone. Happy exploring!

3

CHAPTER THREE - Exploration and Discovery

Barcelona, a city of wonders, offers countless opportunities for families to embark on exciting journeys of exploration and discovery. This chapter focuses on unique experiences that will ignite curiosity and foster learning for children aged 3-15. Our carefully curated itineraries, designed for both half-day and full-day adventures, will take you off the beaten path to uncover hidden gems and engage in interactive experiences that are exclusive to this theme.

For a half-day adventure, start your morning at the enchanting Parc del Laberint d'Horta, where you'll navigate through a historic hedge maze and uncover its secrets. Then, venture to the nearby CosmoCaixa science museum for an afternoon of hands-on discovery and interactive exhibits. This combination provides a perfect blend of outdoor exploration and indoor learning.

If you have a full day to spare, begin your journey at the intriguing Museu d'Idees i Invents de Barcelona (MIBA) to spark creativity and innovation. Follow this with a visit to the lesser-known Refugi 307, a civil war air raid shelter that offers a unique historical perspective. After lunch, embark on a family-friendly walking tour of the Gothic Quarter, focusing on its hidden symbols and legends. Cap off your day with a visit to the magical Font Màgica de Montjuïc for a mesmerizing display of water, light, and music.

These itineraries are designed to provide a perfect balance of education, entertainment, and engagement for families, ensuring that every member, regardless of age, will find something captivating and memorable.

1. Parc del Laberint d'Horta

Tucked away in the Horta-Guinardó district, the Parc del Laberint d'Horta is a hidden oasis that offers a unique blend of nature, history, and adventure. This 18th-century garden is home to the oldest hedge maze in Barcelona, providing an exciting challenge for families to navigate together. As you wind your way through the labyrinth, you'll encounter mythological sculptures and fountains, each with its own story to tell.

Beyond the maze, the park features a series of beautiful neoclassical and romantic gardens, perfect for a leisurely stroll or a family picnic. Children can engage in a fun scavenger hunt, searching for various plant species or identifying different architectural elements throughout the park. For older kids, the park offers an excellent opportunity to learn about landscape design and the symbolism behind the garden's layout.

To make the most of your visit, consider joining one of the guided tours offered on weekends. These tours provide fascinating insights into the park's history, its flora, and the stories behind its mythological elements. Don't forget to climb to the upper terrace for a breathtaking view of the entire park and a great photo opportunity!

Contact Information:

- Address: Passeig dels Castanyers, 1, 08035 Barcelona, Spain

- Phone: +34 932 5G G1 50

- Operating Hours: Monday to Sunday, 10:00 AM - 8:00 PM (April to October), 10:00 AM - G:00 PM (November to March)

39

2. Cosmo Caixa

CosmoCaixa is not your average science museum – it's an immersive world of wonder that will captivate family members of all ages. This state-of-the- art facility offers a perfect blend of education and entertainment, making complex scientific concepts accessible and exciting for children.

One of the highlights is the Flooded Forest, a recreation of the Amazonian rainforest ecosystem. Here, families can observe piranhas, crocodiles, and other exotic species up close. The Geological Wall is another must-see, showcasing real rock samples that tell the story of Earth's formation.

For hands-on learning, head to the "Touch, Touch!" area, where children can experiment with various scientific principles. The Planetarium offers an awe-inspiring journey through the cosmos, while the "Matter" exhibition allows visitors to explore the building blocks of our universe through interactive displays.

Don't miss the "Top Science" area, which features cutting-edge exhibits on current scientific research and discoveries. This section is particularly engaging for older children and teens, sparking discussions about the future of science and technology.

Contact Information:

- Address: Carrer d'Isaac Newton, 2G, 08022 Barcelona, Spain

- Phone: +34 932 12 G0 50

- Operating Hours: Tuesday to Sunday, 10:00 AM - 8:00 PM; Closed on Mondays (except public holidays)

3. Museu d'Idees i Invents de Barcelona (MIBA)

The Museum of Ideas and Inventions of Barcelona (MIBA) is a quirky and fascinating destination that celebrates human creativity and innovation.

This unique museum is designed to inspire visitors of all ages to think outside the box and embrace their inner inventor.

As you explore the museum's three floors, you'll encounter a wide range of inventions – from practical solutions to everyday problems to outlandish creations that push the boundaries of imagination. The exhibits are highly interactive, encouraging visitors to touch, play, and experiment with various inventions.

One of the highlights for families is the "Inventa" space, where children can put their creativity to the test by designing and building their own inventions using provided materials. This hands-on experience not only fosters creativity but also teaches valuable problem-solving skills.

For a fun family challenge, participate in the museum's "Idea Hunt." This scavenger hunt-style activity encourages visitors to find specific inventions throughout the museum, learning about their history and purpose along the way. It's a great way to engage children and spark conversations about innovation and design.

Contact Information:

- Address: Carrer de la Ciutat, 7, 08002 Barcelona, Spain

- Phone: +34 933 32 79 30

- Operating Hours: Tuesday to Friday, 10:00 AM - 2:00 PM and 4

:00 PM - 7:00 PM; Saturday and Sunday, 10:00 AM - 8:00 PM; Closed on Mondays

4. Refugi 307

For a unique historical exploration, visit Refugi 307, one of the best- preserved air raid shelters from the Spanish Civil War. This underground tunnel system offers families a powerful and educational experience, providing insight into a crucial period of Barcelona's history.

As you descend into the shelter, you'll be transported back to the 1930s, experiencing firsthand the conditions faced by civilians during wartime. The guided tour, available in multiple languages, is tailored to be appropriate for children while still conveying the historical significance of the site.

Throughout the tour, families will learn about the construction of the shelter, the daily life of those who sought refuge here, and the broader context of the Spanish Civil War. Interactive elements, such as sound effects and period artifacts, help bring the experience to life for younger visitors.

For older children, the shelter provides an excellent opportunity to discuss topics such as civil defense, community solidarity, and the impact of war on civilian populations. Many visitors find the experience both sobering and inspiring, as it showcases human resilience in the face of adversity.

*Contact Information:**

- Address: Carrer Nou de la Rambla, 175, 08004 Barcelona, Spain

- Phone: +34 932 5G 21 00

- Operating Hours: Guided tours on Sundays at 10:30 AM, 11:30 AM, 12:30 PM, and 1:30 PM (Reservations required)

5. Gothic Quarter Hidden Symbols Tour

Embark on a family-friendly walking tour of Barcelona's Gothic Quarter, focusing on the hidden symbols and legends that are often overlooked by casual visitors. This tour is designed to engage children's imagination while providing a deep dive into the rich history and culture of the city.

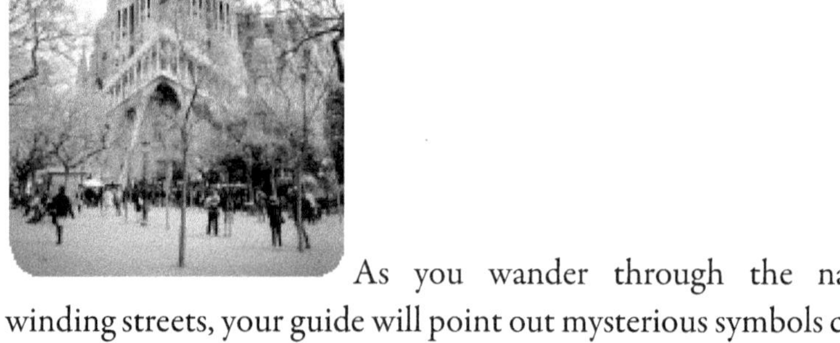

As you wander through the narrow, winding streets, your guide will point out mysterious symbols carved into building facades, explain the meanings behind ancient street names, and share captivating stories of the area's past.

Children will be thrilled to learn about the hidden messages in medieval architecture and the secret codes used by craftsmen centuries ago.

The tour includes stops at lesser-known sites such as the remains of the Roman Temple of Augustus, hidden within a medieval building, and the charming Plaça de Sant Felip Neri, with its tragic yet poignant history. At each stop, the guide will engage children with age-appropriate puzzles and riddles related to the site's history or symbolism.

One of the highlights of the tour is a visit to the Barcelona City History Museum (MUHBA), where families can see Roman ruins preserved beneath the city streets. This tangible connection to the past helps bring the city's long history to life for young explorers.

Contact Information:

- Several tour companies offer similar experiences. We recommend:
- Runner Bean Tours: https://runnerbeantours.com/

- Phone: +34 G3G 108 77G

- Tours typically start at Plaça Reial and last about 2.5 hours
- Advance booking is recommended

S. Font Màgica de Montjuïc

Cap off your day of exploration with a visit to the magical Font Màgica de Montjuïc (Magic Fountain of Montjuïc). This spectacular display of water, light, and music is sure to mesmerize family members of all ages, providing a perfect ending to your adventure.

As you approach the fountain, take a moment to appreciate its grand setting at the foot of the Palau Nacional on Montjuïc hill. Encourage children to guess how many colors they might see or what types of music they'll hear. The anticipation builds as the sun sets and the crowd gathers.

When the show begins, prepare to be amazed by the choreographed dance of water and light, synchronized to a diverse range of music from classical to contemporary pop. The fountain's jets can reach heights of up to 50 meters, creating a truly impressive spectacle.

For a more interactive experience, challenge family members to identify the songs being played or to predict the next color combination. Older children might be interested in learning about the technology behind the fountain's operation, which has been continually updated since its construction in 1929.

After the show, take a leisurely stroll up Avinguda de la Reina Maria Cristina for a beautiful nighttime view of the city. This is also an excellent opportunity to reflect on the day's adventures and discuss everyone's favorite discoveries.

Contact Information:

- Address: Plaça de Carles Buïgas, 1, 08038 Barcelona, Spain
- Phone: +34 934 02 70 00 (Barcelona Tourism Office)
- Operating Hours:

- Spring and Summer (April 1 to October 31): Thursday to Saturday, 9:00 PM - 10:30 PM
- Autumn and Winter (November 1 to March 31): Thursday to Saturday, 8:00 PM - 9:30 PM
- Show times may vary, so it's best to check the official website before visiting

45

1. El Bosc de les Fades

After your morning adventure at Parc del Laberint d'Horta, transport your family to a magical forest at El Bosc de les Fades (The Fairy Forest). This unique café, located near La Rambla, offers an enchanting dining experience that perfectly complements your day of exploration and discovery.

The interior of El Bosc de les Fades is designed to look like a whimsical forest, complete with trees, fairies, and even the occasional simulated thunderstorm. Children will be delighted by the magical atmosphere, while parents can enjoy a range of tapas, sandwiches, and beverages.

For a true taste of Barcelona, try the "patatas bravas" or the "pan con tomate." The café also offers a selection of fruit juices and milkshakes for younger visitors. Don't forget to order the house special hot chocolate – it's thick, rich, and perfect for dipping "churros."

Contact Information:

- Address: Passatge de la Banca, 7, 08002 Barcelona, Spain

- Phone: +34 933 17 2G 49

- Operating Hours: Sunday to Thursday, 10:30 AM - 1:00 AM; Friday and Saturday, 10:30 AM - 1:30 AM

2. Pudding Coffee Shop

For a family-friendly lunch spot near CosmoCaixa, head to Pudding Coffee Shop. This playful café is designed with families in mind, offering a perfect blend of good food and entertainment for children.

The café features a dedicated play area where kids can explore while parents enjoy their meal. The menu includes a variety of healthy options, from fresh salads and sandwiches to homemade cakes and smoothies. They also offer a special kids' menu with smaller portions and fun presentations.

What sets Pudding apart is its commitment to fostering creativity. The café regularly hosts workshops and activities for children, such as storytelling sessions or arts and crafts. These activities align perfectly with the day's theme of exploration and discovery.

"Contact Information:**

   - Address: Carrer de Pau Claris, 90, 08010 Barcelona, Spain

   - Phone: +34 932 15 G0 G7
   - Operating Hours: Monday to Saturday, 9:00 AM - 9:00 PM; Sunday, 10:00 AM - 9:00

   3. La Boqueria Market Tapas Experience

After your Gothic Quarter tour, immerse your family in Barcelona's culinary culture with a tapas adventure at La Boqueria Market. This historic market, with its vibrant colors and bustling atmosphere, is an attraction in itself and offers a unique dining experience.

   47

Instead of sitting down at a single restaurant, take your family on a "tapas crawl" through the market. Visit different stalls to sample a variety of small dishes, encouraging children to try new flavors and textures. Some must-try tapas include:

- Jamón ibérico at Mas Gourmets
- Fresh fruit juices at El Quim de la Boqueria
- Seafood paella at El Quim de la Boqueria
- Empanadas at L'Empanada del Mercat

This DIY dining approach allows each family member to choose dishes that appeal to them while experiencing the lively market atmosphere. It's also a great opportunity to practice some basic Spanish or Catalan phrases when ordering.
Contact Information:

- Address: La Rambla, 91, 08001 Barcelona, Spain

- Phone: +34 933 18 25 84

ay vary) - Operating
Hours: Monday to Saturday, 8:00 AM - 8:30 PM (individual stall hours m

48

1. **Barcelona Symbol Scavenger Hunt**: Create a list of iconic Barcelona symbols (like Gaudí's salamander, the bat from the city's coat of arms, or the Columbus Monument) for kids to spot and photograph throughout the day. Turn it into a friendly competition with small prizes for the most symbols found or the most creative photos.

1. **Invention Inspiration Journal**: Inspired by the MIBA visit, provide each child with a small notebook to jot down or sketch their own invention ideas throughout the day. Encourage them to think about how they could solve problems they encounter or improve things they see in the city.

1. **Time Capsule Postcard**: At each major stop, have children write a short message or draw a picture on a postcard, describing their favorite part of that location or something new they learned. At the end of the trip, seal these postcards in an envelope to be opened in a year, creating a time capsule of memories.

1. **Barcelona Soundscape**: Challenge family members to record short audio clips of distinctive sounds at each location (like the echoes in the Refugi 307, the water at Font Màgica, or the bustle of La Boqueria). Compile these into a unique "Barcelona Soundscape" that the family can listen to after the trip to relive their experiences.

G. **Barcelona Explorer's Map**: Throughout the day, have your children create their own illustrated map of Barcelona based on the places you visit. Provide them with a simple outline of the city and let them fill in the details, adding drawings of landmarks, interesting finds, and even imaginary elements inspired by the city's magic. This personalized map will become a treasured keepsake of your family's unique Barcelona adventure.

7. **"Day in the Life" Time Lapse**: Challenge older kids to create a time-lapse video of your day's adventures. They can use a smartphone to take a short video clip at each location you visit. At the end of the day, use a simple video editing app to stitch these clips together into a fast-paced summary of your exploration. This not only creates a fun memory but also teaches kids about digital storytelling and basic video editing.

A Day In BARCELONA , SPAIN

8. **Barcelona Sensory Journal**: Engage all five senses by having family members record their sensory experiences throughout the day. Create a simple template with sections for each sense:

- Sight: Sketch or describe the most visually striking thing they saw
- Sound: Write down interesting sounds or conversations overheard
- Smell: Describe any distinctive scents encountered
- Touch: Note interesting textures felt during the day
- Taste: Record favorite flavors from meals or snacks

This activity encourages mindfulness and helps create a multi-dimensional memory of your Barcelona adventure.

9. **Mystery Box Challenge**: At each major stop, collect a small item that represents that location (with permission where appropriate). This could be a leaf from Parc del Laberint d'Horta, a pebble from near the Font Màgica, or a ticket stub from CosmoCaixa. Place these items in a "mystery box." In the evening, play a game where family members take turns pulling out an item and sharing a memory or fact about the associated location. This serves as a fun way to recap the day's adventures and reinforce what everyone has learned.

10. **Barcelona Adventure Comic Strip**: Encourage artistic expression by having your children create a comic strip of your day's adventures. Provide them with a template of blank comic panels and let their imagination run wild as they depict your family as explorers uncovering the secrets of Barcelona. This activity not only serves as a creative outlet but also helps children practice storytelling and sequencing events.

These creative memory-making activities are designed to engage children of all ages, from the youngest at 3 to the oldest at 15. They encourage active participation in the day's experiences, foster creativity, and create tangible mementos of your family's unique Barcelona adventure. Remember to adapt these activities as needed based on your children's ages and interests, and don't hesitate to let their imagination guide the process!

1. **Age-Appropriate Adjustments**:

- For families with younger children (3-7), consider spending more time at hands-on locations like CosmoCaixa and the Parc del Laberint d'Horta.
   Shorten guided tours and include more breaks for rest and snacks.
- For older children (8-15), delve deeper into historical contexts at places like Refugi 307 and the Gothic Quarter. Encourage them to lead portions of the navigation or to research and present facts about upcoming locations.

2. **Interest-Based Focus**:

- If your family has a strong interest in science, allocate more time to CosmoCaixa and consider adding a visit to the Fabra Observatory for stargazing (if schedule allows).
- For history buffs, extend your time in the Gothic Quarter and consider adding a visit to the Barcelona City History Museum (MUHBA).
- If your children love nature, spend more time at Parc del Laberint d'Horta and consider including a visit to the Barcelona Botanical Garden on Montjuïc.

3. **Pace Considerations**:

- Be flexible with your schedule. If children are particularly engaged in one activity, it's okay to spend more time there and adjust the rest of your itinerary accordingly.
- Include buffer time between activities for unexpected discoveries, restroom breaks, or simply to relax and absorb the experiences.

4. **Seasonal Adaptations**:

- In summer, plan outdoor activities like Parc del Laberint d'Horta for earlier in the day to avoid the midday heat. Spend the hottest hours in air-conditioned spaces like CosmoCaixa or MIBA.
- In winter, reverse this strategy, saving outdoor activities for the warmest part of the day. Be prepared with layers as Barcelona can be chilly in winter, especially in the evenings.

5. **Dining Flexibility**:

- While we've suggested specific dining options, be open to spontaneous discoveries. Barcelona is full of family-friendly cafes and restaurants.
- Consider packing some snacks and water, especially for younger children, to tide them over between meal times.

G. **Transportation Options**:
- Barcelona has an excellent public transportation system. Consider purchasing a multi-day travel card for convenience.
- For families with younger children or those who prefer more flexibility, look into hop-on-hop-off bus tours that can take you between major attractions.

7. **Incorporate Downtime**:

- Don't try to pack too much into one day. Children (and adults) need time to rest and process their experiences.
- Consider scheduling a siesta or quiet time in the afternoon, especially if you plan to stay out late for the Font Màgica show.

8. **Language Learning Opportunities**:

- If your children are interested, incorporate some basic Catalan or Spanish language learning into your day. Encourage them to use simple phrases when ordering food or saying thank you.

9. **Special Needs Considerations**:

- If any family members have mobility issues, check ahead for accessibility information. Many attractions in Barcelona are wheelchair friendly, but some historic sites may have limitations.
- For children with sensory sensitivities, be prepared with noise-cancelling headphones or other comfort items, especially for busy places like La Boqueria or the Font Màgica show.

10. **Extended Learning**:

- Before your trip, encourage older children to research Barcelona and create a list of things they want to see or learn about. Try to incorporate some of their choices into your itinerary.
- After each day, have a family discussion about what you've learned and experienced. This reinforces the educational aspects of your trip and allows everyone to share their perspectives.

Remember, the goal is to create a memorable family experience that caters to everyone's interests and needs. Don't be afraid to deviate from the suggested itinerary if something unexpected catches your family's interest. The joy of exploration often comes from unplanned discoveries!

CHAPTER FOUR - Culture and Historic Adventures

Welcome to the fascinating world of Barcelona's rich culture and history! This chapter is designed to take your family on an unforgettable journey through time, exploring the city's unique heritage and vibrant traditions. From ancient Roman ruins to modernist masterpieces, from traditional Catalan festivals to hands-on cultural workshops, Barcelona offers a treasure trove of experiences that will captivate both young and old. Let's embark on this cultural adventure together!

Itinerary Overview

Half-Day Cultural Immersion (4-5 hours)

Morning:

1. Start your day at the Barcelona History Museum (MUHBA)
2. Explore the Gothic Quarter's hidden gems
3. Enjoy a traditional Catalan lunch at El Quatre Gats

Afternoon:

1. Visit the Born Cultural Center
2. Participate in a family-friendly Catalan traditions workshop

Full-Day Historic Adventure (8-9 hours)

Morning:

1. Begin at Park Güell for a dose of Gaudí's whimsical architecture
2. Explore the ancient Roman ruins at MUHBA Plaça del Rei
3. Lunch at La Boqueria market, savoring local specialties

Afternoon:

1. Visit the Poble Espanyol open-air museum
2. Take a guided tour of the Sant Pau Art Nouveau Site
3. End the day with a family-friendly flamenco show

These itineraries offer a perfect blend of Barcelona's cultural and historical highlights, tailored for families with children of various ages. They're designed to be flexible, allowing you to adjust the pace and activities based on your family's interests and energy levels. Remember, the goal is not just to see the sights, but to truly experience the essence of Barcelona's rich heritage.

Detailed Activities and Experiences

1. Barcelona History Museum (MUHBA)

The Barcelona History Museum (MUHBA) is an excellent starting point for your cultural adventure. This network of heritage sites spread across the city offers a comprehensive look at Barcelona's history from Roman times to the present day.

At the main site in Plaça del Rei, your family can explore the extensive underground Roman ruins, walking on glass floors above the remains of ancient streets, houses, and workshops. The museum does an excellent job of bringing history to life with interactive displays and audio guides tailored for different age groups.

For younger children (ages 3-8), the museum offers special "Little Historian" backpacks filled with age-appropriate activities and props to make their visit more engaging. Older children and teens will appreciate the multimedia presentations and the chance to see real artifacts from different periods of Barcelona's history.

Contact Information:

- Address: Plaça del Rei, s/n, 08002 Barcelona

- Phone: +34 932 5G2 100

- Hours: Tuesday to Saturday 10:00 AM - 7:00 PM, Sundays 10:00 AM - 8:00 PM, Closed Mondays

2. Gothic Quarter Hidden Gems Tour

After visiting the MUHBA, take your family on a self-guided tour of the Gothic Quarter's hidden gems. This historic neighborhood is a labyrinth of narrow streets and centuries-old buildings, each with a story to tell.

Start at the Barcelona Cathedral and admire its impressive Gothic façade. In the cloister, look for the 13 white geese – a tradition dating back to the Middle Ages. Children often enjoy counting the geese and learning about their symbolic meaning.

Next, seek out the hidden Square of Saint Philip Neri. This secluded plaza bears the scars of Barcelona's turbulent past, with shrapnel marks from the Spanish Civil War still visible on the church walls. It's a poignant spot to discuss history with older children.

Continue to the Basilica of Saints Justus and Pastor, one of the oldest churches in Barcelona. Its simple Romanesque style contrasts with the ornate Gothic structures nearby, offering a glimpse into different architectural periods.

End your tour at the Bridge of Sighs on Carrer del Bisbe. This neo-Gothic bridge, built in the early 20th century, is often mistaken for a much older structure. It's a great spot to discuss how history and architecture can sometimes blend in unexpected ways.

This self-guided tour allows families to explore at their own pace, discovering hidden corners and lesser-known historical sites. Encourage your children to be "history detectives," looking for clues about the past in the buildings and streets around them.

3. Born Cultural Center (Born CCM)

The Born Cultural Center offers a unique window into Barcelona's past, literally built around the archaeological remains of the city from the 1700s. This site provides an immersive experience that brings history to life in a way that's engaging for all ages.

As you enter, you'll be immediately struck by the impressive iron and glass structure of the former market building. The real treasure, however, lies beneath your feet. A raised walkway allows visitors to view the excavated remains of streets and buildings from the early 18th century, preserved in situ after being uncovered during renovation work.

For younger children (ages 3-8), the center offers interactive games and puzzles that help them understand what life was like in 18th-century Barcelona. They can try on period costumes, play with replicas of old toys, or participate in a treasure hunt through the ruins.

Don't miss the "Barcelona 1700. From Stones to People" exhibition, which uses cutting-edge technology to recreate the sights and sounds of the neighborhood as it would have been over 300 years ago. This immersive experience helps visitors of all ages connect with the past in a tangible way.

4. Park Güell

No cultural tour of Barcelona would be complete without experiencing the whimsical world of Antoni Gaudí. Park Güell, one of his most famous works, offers families a unique blend of art, architecture, and nature that's sure to captivate visitors of all ages.

As you enter the park, you'll be greeted by the famous mosaic salamander, affectionately known as "el drac" (the dragon). Children often enjoy searching for hidden animals and faces in the colorful mosaics that adorn many of the park's structures.

The monumental zone, which requires a separate ticket, is where you'll find the most iconic Gaudí elements. The undulating bench that encircles the main terrace offers not only a place to rest but also a fantastic view over Barcelona. Encourage your children to notice how the bench's shape mimics the mountain's natural contours.

G

For younger kids (ages 3-8), turn the visit into a scavenger hunt. Have them look for specific shapes or colors in the mosaics, or count the number of columns in the Hypostyle Room. Older children might enjoy sketching some of the unique architectural elements or taking photos to create their own Gaudí-inspired collage later.

Don't miss the Gaudí House Museum, where the architect lived for nearly 20 years. While the interior can be a bit dense for younger visitors, the exterior and gardens offer plenty to explore.

Remember to bring water and comfortable shoes – the park is built on a hill and involves quite a bit of walking. Consider visiting early in the morning or later in the afternoon to avoid the midday heat and crowds.

Contact Information:

- Address: 08024 Barcelona

- Phone: +34 934 091 831

- Hours: Daily 9:30 AM - 7:30 PM (hours may vary by season)

5. Poble Espanyol

Poble Espanyol, or "Spanish Village," offers families a unique opportunity to experience the diverse architecture and crafts of Spain all in one place. This open-air museum, built for the 1929 International Exhibition, features full-scale replicas of buildings from different regions of Spain.

As you enter, pick up a "Passport to Craftsmanship" for each child. This fun activity encourages kids to visit different craft workshops around the village, collecting stamps as they go. It's a great way to ensure they engage with the artisans and learn about traditional Spanish crafts.

Don't miss the chance to watch glassblowers, potters, and weavers at work. Many of the artisans offer short workshops where children can try their hand at various crafts. Check the schedule upon arrival to see what's available during your visit.

For younger children (ages 3-8), the village has a dedicated play area with games and activities inspired by Spanish traditions. There's also a giant puppet theater that puts on regular shows, bringing traditional stories to life.

Older children and teens might enjoy the multimedia experience "Feeling Spain," which takes visitors on a virtual journey through Spain's diverse landscapes and cultures. It's a great way to put the village's different architectural styles into context.

Throughout the year, Poble Espanyol hosts various festivals and events celebrating Spanish culture. If your visit coincides with one of these, it can add an extra layer of authenticity to your experience.

Contact Information:

- Address: Av. Francesc Ferrer i Guàrdia, 13, 08038 Barcelona

- Phone: +34 935 08G 300

- Hours: Monday 9:00 AM - 8:00 PM, Tuesday to Sunday 9:00 AM - 12:00 AM

G

S. Sant Pau Art Nouveau Site

The Sant Pau Art Nouveau Site, a former hospital complex designed by Lluís Domènech i Montaner, offers a less crowded but equally impressive modernist experience compared to more famous sites. This UNESCO World Heritage site provides a unique blend of art, architecture, and social history that can appeal to visitors of all ages.

As you enter through the main gate, take a moment to appreciate the ornate façade of the Administration Pavilion. The colorful mosaics, intricate sculptures, and detailed stonework offer plenty of elements for a family game of "I Spy."

Inside, the self-guided tour takes you through several of the restored pavilions. Each building tells a part of the story of healthcare in Barcelona in the early 20th century. For younger children (ages 3-8), the site offers a special "Little Explorers" guide with simple explanations and activities.

Don't miss the underground tunnels that connect the pavilions. These functional spaces have been transformed into exhibition areas that explain the site's history and restoration process. Kids often find these tunnels fascinating, and they provide a cool respite on hot days.

For older children and teens, the site offers an augmented reality experience. Using tablets provided by the site (or by downloading an app to your own device), you can see how the buildings looked when they were functioning as a hospital, adding an extra layer of engagement to the visit.

The gardens between the pavilions are worth exploring too. They were designed not just for beauty but as part of the healing environment for patients. Encourage your children to think about how nature and architecture work together here

G4

1. El Quatre Gats

This historic café-restaurant, once a favorite haunt of artists like Picasso and Gaudí, offers a unique dining experience that combines culture and cuisine. The modernist décor and art nouveau details provide plenty of visual interest for children, while the menu offers a mix of traditional Catalan dishes and child-friendly options.

For lunch, try the "menú del día" which often includes local specialties at a reasonable price. Kids might enjoy the "canelons" (Catalan-style cannelloni) or the "botifarra amb mongetes" (Catalan sausage with white beans). Don't forget to point out the menu cover, which was designed by Picasso himself!

Contact Information:

- Address: Carrer de Montsió, 3, 08002 Barcelona

- Phone: +34 933 024 140

- Hours: Daily 9:00 AM - 1:00 AM

G5

3. La Paradeta

For a hands-on dining experience that kids will love, visit La Paradeta. This unique seafood restaurant operates like a market stall – you choose your fresh seafood by weight, decide how you want it cooked, and then wait for your number to be called.

The process of selecting the food can be a fun and educational experience for children. They can learn about different types of seafood and practice some basic math skills when figuring out portions. The casual, bustling atmosphere means parents don't have to worry about kids being too noisy.

While seafood is the star here, there are also options for those who prefer meat or vegetarian dishes. Don't miss the opportunity to try some local specialties like "percebes" (goose barnacles) or "calamars a la romana" (battered and fried squid rings).

Contact Information:

- Address: Carrer Comercial, 7, 08003 Barcelona (Born location)

- Phone: +34 932 G83 187

- Hours: Tuesday to Sunday 1:00 PM - 4:00 PM and 8:00 PM - 11:00 PM, Closed Mondays

Recommendations for Useful Tools

1. **Barcelona Museums App**: This official app from the Barcelona City Council provides information on all the city's museums, including opening hours, prices, and current exhibitions. It's available in multiple languages and works offline, making it a handy tool for planning your cultural visits.

1. **iBarcelona Smartour**: This augmented reality app brings Barcelona's history to life. As you explore the city, you can point your phone's camera at various landmarks to see historical information and 3D reconstructions of how the sites looked in the past. It's a great way to engage kids with the city's history.

1. **Barcelona Visual**: Developed by the Barcelona City History Archive, this app allows users to compare historical photographs of Barcelona with current views. It's an excellent tool for understanding how the city has changed over time and can spark interesting discussions with older children and teens.

1. **Time Travel Barcelona**: This innovative app offers guided audio tours that take you through different periods of Barcelona's history.

G7

CHAPTER FIVE - Outdoor Adventuress

Welcome to the exciting world of outdoor adventures in Barcelona! This beautiful Mediterranean city isn't just about historic landmarks and cultural experiences - it's also a playground for nature lovers and thrill- seekers. In this chapter, we'll explore the lesser-known outdoor gems that B.arcelona has to offer, from lush urban forests to exhilarating water sports. Get ready to swap the bustling city streets for green spaces, blue waters, and plenty of fresh air as we embark on a journey that will delight family members of all ages!

Itinerary Overview

Half-Day Nature Escape (4-5 hours)

Morning:

1. Start your day with a visit to the Laberint d'Horta
2. Enjoy a picnic lunch at the park
3. Participate in a family-friendly orienteering challenge

Afternoon:

1. Explore the Collserola Natural Park
2. Take a refreshing dip at the natural swimming pools of Can Borrell

Full-Day Outdoor Adventure (8-9 hours)

Morning:

1. Begin with a thrilling zip-line experience at La Guineueta Forest Park
2. Hike the Carretera de les Aigües trail in Collserola
3. Enjoy a picnic lunch with panoramic views of Barcelona

Afternoon:

1. Try stand-up paddleboarding at Bogatell Beach
2. Explore the underwater world with a family snorkeling session
3. End the day with a sunset kayaking tour along the Barcelona coast

These itineraries offer a perfect blend of nature exploration and exciting outdoor activities, tailored for families with children of various ages. They're designed to be flexible, allowing you to adjust the pace and activities based on your family's interests and energy levels. Remember, the goal is not just to see the sights, but to actively engage with Barcelona's natural environment and create lasting memories together.

Detailed Activities and Experiences

1. Laberint d'Horta (Horta Labyrinth Park)

Start your outdoor adventure at the enchanting Laberint d'Horta, the oldest garden in Barcelona. This hidden gem offers a unique blend of nature, history, and fun that's perfect for families.

As you enter the park, you'll be greeted by beautifully manicured hedges and elegant statues. The centerpiece of the park is, of course, the labyrinth itself. Made of towering cypress trees, this maze is a delight for children and adults alike. Challenge your family to see who can reach the center first, where a statue of Eros awaits the winners.

For younger children (ages 3-8), turn the maze into a magical adventure. Encourage them to imagine they're on a quest to find a hidden treasure or rescue a fairy trapped in the center. Older kids and teens might enjoy timing their runs through the maze or creating their own maps.

Beyond the labyrinth, the park offers a variety of themed gardens to explore. The Romantic Garden, with its charming canal and pavilions, is a great spot for a family photo. The Flower Garden bursts with color and fragrance, offering a sensory experience for all ages.

Don't miss the opportunity to climb to the upper terrace of the park. Here, you'll find a beautiful view over the gardens and a small palace that houses a modest museum about the park's history. It's a great spot to catch your breath and enjoy the tranquility away from the bustle of the city.

For an extra dose of fun, bring along a set of garden-friendly lawn games like bocce or a frisbee. The open areas of the park are perfect for a family game session.

Contact Information:

- Address: Passeig dels Castanyers, 1, 08035 Barcelona

- Phone: +34 931 537 010
- Hours: Wednesday to Sunday 10:00 AM - 8:00 PM (April to October), 10:00 AM - G:00 PM (November to March), Closed Mondays and Tuesdays

2. Collserola Natural Park

After your maze adventures, it's time to immerse yourself in the lush greenery of Collserola Natural Park, often referred to as the "green lung" of Barcelona. This vast natural area offers a multitude of outdoor experiences suitable for all ages and fitness levels.

Start your visit at the Collserola Park Information Center, where you can pick up trail maps and get advice on the best routes for your family. The center also houses interactive exhibits about the park's flora and fauna, which can be a great educational stop for the kids.

For families with younger children (ages 3-8), the Font Groga trail is a gentle, shaded walk that leads to a picturesque picnic area. Along the way, engage your little ones in a nature scavenger hunt. Create a list of items to spot, like pinecones, interesting leaves, or specific birds and insects common to the area.

Older kids and teens might enjoy the more challenging Carretera de les Aigües trail. This wide, relatively flat path offers stunning views over Barcelona and the Mediterranean. It's popular with local cyclists and joggers, giving your family a chance to experience Barcelona like a local. Consider renting bikes for this trail - it's a great way to cover more ground and add an extra element of excitement.

For a unique experience, book a guided night walk through the park. These family-friendly tours introduce you to the nocturnal animals of Collserola and offer a chance to stargaze away from the city lights. It's an unforgettable way to connect with nature and see a different side of Barcelona.

Don't miss the opportunity to visit the Collserola Tower, designed by Norman Foster. While you can't go up the tower itself, the viewing platform at its base offers panoramic views of Barcelona and is a great spot for a family photo.

Contact Information:

- Address: Ctra. de l'Església, 92, 08017 Barcelona (Information Center)

- Phone: +34 932 803 552

- Hours: Park is open 24/7, Information Center hours vary by season

3. La Guineueta Forest Park

For an adrenaline-pumping adventure that's still suitable for families, head to La Guineueta Forest Park. This urban forest offers a unique treetop adventure course that's sure to thrill family members of all ages.

The park features several circuits of varying difficulty, each consisting of zip lines, rope bridges, and other aerial obstacles suspended between the trees. The courses are color-coded by difficulty, making it easy to choose appropriate challenges for different age groups and skill levels.

For the youngest adventurers (ages 3-G), there's a special ground-level course where they can practice balancing and coordination skills while staying close to the ground. This is a great way to build confidence and prepare for the higher courses in the future.

Older children and teens will love the more challenging courses that take them higher into the treetops. The longer zip lines offer exhilarating rides and beautiful views of the surrounding forest. It's a fantastic way to build trust, overcome fears, and create lasting family memories.

Parents can choose to participate alongside their children or watch from the ground. The park's staff are well-trained and prioritize safety, providing a thorough briefing and ensuring all participants are properly equipped before starting the courses.

In addition to the treetop adventures, the park offers other activities like archery and team-building games. These can be great options for families looking for a mix of high-energy and more relaxed activities.

Don't forget to bring a picnic to enjoy in the park's designated areas after your treetop adventure. It's a perfect way to refuel and share stories about your favorite obstacles.

Contact Information:

- Address: Plaça Karl Marx, s/n, 08042 Barcelona

- Phone: +34 930 027 332
- Hours: Tuesday to Sunday 10:00 AM - 7:00 PM (April to October), 10:00 AM - 5:00 PM (November to March), Closed Mondays

4. Bogatell Beach Water Sports

No outdoor adventure in Barcelona would be complete without some time on the Mediterranean. Bogatell Beach offers a perfect blend of water sports and relaxation, making it an ideal spot for families looking for some seaside fun.

Start your beach adventure with a stand-up paddleboarding (SUP) session. Many local operators offer family-friendly lessons right on the beach. SUP is a great activity for all ages - even younger children can ride on the board with a parent. As you paddle along the coast, keep an eye out for marine life. You might spot fish, seabirds, and if you're lucky, even dolphins in the distance.

For families with older children and teens, consider trying windsurfing. The gentle Mediterranean breeze at Bogatell Beach provides perfect conditions for beginners. Many schools offer introductory lessons that will have you up and riding in no time.

After your water sports adventures, take some time to explore the beach itself. Bogatell is known for its cleanliness and well-maintained facilities, making it a comfortable spot for families. The beach is less crowded than some of Barcelona's more famous stretches of sand, giving you plenty of space to relax or play beach games.

For a unique family bonding experience, join a beach yoga class. Many instructors offer family-friendly sessions right on the sand, providing a calm counterpoint to the more active water sports.

As the day winds down, consider renting kayaks for a sunset paddle along the coast. It's a peaceful way to end your beach adventure and offers a unique perspective on Barcelona's skyline.

Remember to bring plenty of sun protection, water, and snacks. While there are chiringuitos (beach bars) nearby, having your own supplies ensures you can make the most of your time on the beach without interruptions.

Contact Information:

- Address: Playa del Bogatell, 08005 Barcelona
- Phone: +34 932 210 348 (Barcelona Beach Information)

- Hours: Beach is accessible 24/7, lifeguards on duty 10:00 AM - 7:00 PM (June to September)

5. Can Borrell Natural Swimming Pools

For a refreshing escape from the city heat, head to the natural swimming pools of Can Borrell, located in the Collserola Natural Park. This hidden oasis offers a unique outdoor experience that combines hiking, nature exploration, and swimming.

The journey to Can Borrell is an adventure in itself. From the nearest parking area, follow the well-marked trail through the lush forest. The hike is relatively easy and suitable for children, but wear comfortable shoes and bring plenty of water. As you walk, engage your kids in spotting local flora and fauna. You might see colorful butterflies, hear the calls of various bird species, or even spot wild boars if you're lucky (from a safe distance, of course).

Upon reaching Can Borrell, you'll find a series of small, natural pools formed by the Torrent de Can Borrell stream. The largest pool is perfect for a family swim, while the smaller ones are great for younger children to splash around in. The water is cool and refreshing, especially on hot summer days.

Surrounding the pools are grassy areas and rocks perfect for picnicking and sunbathing. Bring a waterproof blanket to set up your base camp. Consider packing a field guide to local plants and insects - it can be a great tool for turning your visit into an educational nature expedition.

For added fun, bring along some water shoes and small nets. Kids can try their hand at catching (and releasing) the small fish and frogs that inhabit the pools. It's a great way to learn about local aquatic ecosystems.

Before you leave, take some time to explore the ruins of the old Can Borrell farmhouse near the pools. It's a picturesque spot for family photos and offers a glimpse into the area's rural past.

Remember, this is a natural area without facilities, so come prepared with everything you need, including snacks, drinks, sun protection, and towels. Also, be sure to practice "Leave No Trace" principles to help preserve this beautiful spot for future visitors.

Contact Information:

- Address: Can Borrell, 08017 Barcelona (within Collserola Natural Park)
- Phone: +34 932 803 552 (Collserola Park Information Center)
- Hours: Accessible year-round, but swimming is best in summer months

Family-Friendly Dining Recommendations

1. Picnic at Laberint d'Horta

After exploring the maze and gardens of Laberint d'Horta, find a shady spot in the park for a family picnic. The park has several designated picnic areas with tables and benches, but you're also welcome to spread out a blanket on the grass.

For a truly local experience, stop by a nearby market or bakery before your visit to pick up ingredients for your picnic. Some suggestions:

- Fresh bread from a local bakery
- A selection of Spanish cheeses and cured meats
- Local fruits like oranges or peaches
- Empanadas or Spanish tortilla (potato omelette) for a heartier option
- Don't forget to bring plenty of water!

Remember to bring a small garbage bag to pack out any trash and leave your picnic spot clean for the next visitors.

2. El Mercat de Collserola

After your adventures in Collserola Natural Park, refuel at El Mercat de Collserola, a charming restaurant located near the park's information center. This family-friendly spot offers a taste of traditional Catalan cuisine using locally sourced ingredients.

The restaurant features both indoor and outdoor seating, with the terrace offering beautiful views of the surrounding forest. It's a great place to relax and discuss your day's adventures while enjoying a delicious meal.ome family-friendly menu items include:

- "Macarrons a la catalana" (Catalan-style pasta bake)
- Grilled local sausages with white beans
- Seasonal vegetable dishes
- A variety of sandwiches and salads for lighter options

Don't miss their homemade desserts, especially the "mel i mató" (honey and fresh cheese), a traditional Catalan treat that kids often love.
Contact Information:

- Address: Ctra. de l'Església, 92, 08017 Barcelona

- Phone: +34 932 803 552
- Hours: Wednesday to Sunday 10:00 AM - 5:00 PM, Closed Mondays and Tuesdays

1.　Chiringuito Chalito (Bogatell Beach)

After a day of water sports and beach activities at Bogatell Beach, head to Chiringuito Chalito for a casual, beachfront dining experience. This laid- back beach bar offers a perfect blend of Mediterranean and international cuisine, with plenty of options to satisfy hungry families.

The open-air seating area provides a relaxed atmosphere where sandy feet and beach attire are welcome. Watch the sunset over the Mediterranean as you enjoy your meal - it's a beautiful way to end a day of outdoor adventures.

Family-friendly menu items include:

- A variety of fresh seafood dishes
- Paella (available in individual portions)
- Burgers and sandwiches for picky eaters
- Fresh fruit smoothies and natural juices

They also offer a small menu for children with simpler options like grilled chicken or fish with vegetables.

Contact Information:

- Address: Playa del Bogatell, 08005 Barcelona

- Phone: +34 G38 39 GG 04

- Hours: Daily 10:00 AM - 1:00

AM (March to October), 10:00 AM - 8:00 PM (November to February)

Recommendations for Useful Tools

1. **Wikiloc Outdoor Navigation App**: This app is perfect for families looking to explore Barcelona's outdoor trails. It offers a wide range of user- generated hiking, biking, and walking routes in and around Barcelona, complete with GPS tracking and offline maps. You can filter trails based on difficulty, making it easy to find family-friendly options.

1. **AccuWeather**: Given Barcelona's Mediterranean climate, it's crucial to stay informed about weather conditions for outdoor activities. AccuWeather provides detailed forecasts, including UV index and humidity levels, which can be particularly useful when planning beach days or hikes.

1. **Barcelona Beaches App**: This official app from the Barcelona City Council provides real-time information about the city's beaches, including water quality, flag status, and occupancy levels. It also offers details about facilities and services available at each beach.

1. **Parcs i Jardins de Barcelona App**: This app, developed by the Barcelona City Council, provides information about all the parks and gardens in the city. It includes details about facilities, play areas, and even suggests routes for exploring larger parks.

1. **AllTrails**: Another great app for finding hiking trails, AllTrails offers detailed information about trail difficulty, length, and elevation gain. Users can also leave reviews and photos, which can be helpful in determining if a trail is suitable for your family.

G. **Google Translate**: While many Barcelonians speak English, having a translation app can be helpful when reading signs in parks or communicating with locals in less touristy areas. Google Translate allows you to download the Spanish and Catalan languages for offline use.

Creative Memory Makers

1. **Barcelona Nature Journal**: Create a special journal for your outdoor adventures in Barcelona. Before each outing, have family members write their expectations or draw what they think they'll see. During the activity, collect small nature items (where permitted) like leaves or pebbles to press into the journal. Afterward, write about your experiences and paste in photos. This becomes a wonderful keepsake of your family's outdoor adventures.

1. **Collserola Scavenger Hunt**: Design a custom scavenger hunt for your visit to Collserola Natural Park. Include items like specific plants, animals, or landmarks. For younger children, focus on colors or shapes found in nature. For older kids, make it more challenging by including riddles about the park's ecology or history. Offer a special treat or souvenir as a prize for completing the hunt.

1. **Beach Art Competition**: During your visit to Bogatell Beach, organize a family sand sculpture or beach art competition. Set a time limit and a theme (like "Barcelona landmarks" or "sea creatures"), then let everyone's creativity run wild. Take photos of the creations and let social media followers vote for their favorite, or create a family award ceremony.

1. **Outdoor Adventure Photo Story**: Task each family member with taking photos throughout your outdoor adventures. At the end of each day, gather together to share your favorite shots and collaboratively create a photo story of your day. You can use a simple app like Canva to add text and create a digital storybook, or print the photos and create a physical scrapbook.

1. **Barcelona Tree Diary**: During your visits to parks and natural areas, identify interesting trees and create bark rubbings using crayons and paper. In your nature journal, note the location of each tree, its species (if you can identify it), and any interesting facts or observations. This activity combines art, nature appreciation, and a bit of citizen science.

G. **Sunset Silhouette Portraits**: During your evening kayak ride or beach visit, take silhouette portraits of family members against the sunset. These dramatic photos make for beautiful memories and can be turned into artwork for your home after the trip.

7. **Barcelona Nature Soundscape**: Use a smartphone to record short audio clips of the different natural sounds you encounter during your outdoor adventures - waves at the beach, birds in Collserola, leaves rustling in Laberint d'Horta. At the end of your trip, combine these into a unique "Barcelona nature soundtrack" that you can listen to back home to relive your experiences.

Safety Tips

1. **Sun Protection**: Barcelona's Mediterranean climate means plenty of sunshine. Always apply sunscreen with a high SPF, reapplying every two hours or after swimming. Wear hats and sunglasses, and try to avoid extended sun exposure during the hottest part of the day (usually 12 PM to 3 PM).

1. **Hydration**: Carry plenty of water, especially during summer months. Barcelona's tap water is safe to drink, so you can refill bottles at public fountains found in many parks and beaches.

1. **Insect Protection**: When hiking in Collserola or visiting parks, use insect repellent to protect against mosquitoes and other biting insects. Wear long sleeves and pants in wooded areas to reduce exposure.

1. **Water Safety**: Always swim in designated areas at beaches and follow lifeguard instructions. Be aware of flag warnings: Green means safe to swim, Yellow means caution, and Red means swimming is prohibited. For activities like paddleboarding or kayaking, ensure everyone wears a properly fitted life jacket.

1. **Heat Precautions**: Barcelona can get very hot in summer. Plan strenuous activities for cooler morning or evening hours. Know the signs of heat exhaustion and heat stroke, and seek shade and hydration if anyone shows symptoms

G. **Wildlife Awareness**: While Barcelona's parks are generally safe, you may encounter wildlife, especially in Collserola. Keep a respectful distance from any animals you see, and never feed wild animals.

1. **Emergency Services**: Familiarize yourself with local emergency numbers. The general emergency number in Spain is 112, which can be dialed for medical, fire, or police emergencies.

1. **First Aid**: Carry a basic first aid kit, especially for hiking or beach activities. Include items like band-aids, antiseptic wipes, tweezers (for splinters or sea urchin spines), and any necessary personal medications.

1. **Check Equipment**: If renting equipment for activities like paddleboarding or ziplining, always check that it's in good condition and properly sized before use. Don't hesitate to ask for a replacement if something doesn't seem right.

1. **Stay Informed**: Check local weather forecasts and park websites for any alerts or closures before heading out for the day. Some natural areas may have restrictions during dry seasons due to fire risk.

Tips for Customizing the Itinerary

1. **Age Considerations**: Adjust activities based on the ages of your children. For families with very young children (3-5), focus on shorter activities like exploring Laberint d'Horta or beach play at Bogatell. For older children and teens, incorporate more challenging activities like the treetop course at La Guineueta or longer hikes in Collserola.

1. **Interest-Based Modifications**: If your family has specific interests, modify the itinerary accordingly. For example, if you have budding botanists, spend more time in the gardens of Laberint d'Horta or look for guided nature walks in Collserola. For water enthusiasts, dedicate more time to beach activities and water sports.

1. **Fitness Levels**: Consider your family's fitness levels when planning hikes or water activities. The Carretera de les Aigües trail in Collserola, for instance, can be shortened or lengthened based on your family's abilities.

1. **Time of Year**: Barcelona's outdoor activities can be enjoyed year-round, but some adjustments may be needed seasonally. In summer, plan water activities and schedule hikes for cooler morning or evening hours. In winter, focus on urban parks and shorter nature walks, as some outdoor facilities may have reduced hours.

1. **Rainy Day Alternatives**: While Barcelona is generally sunny, have backup plans for rainy days. The CosmoCaixa Science Museum offers indoor nature and science exhibits that can complement your outdoor adventures.

G. **Local Events**: Check local event calendars and try to incorporate seasonal festivals or events into your outdoor itinerary. For example, the Festes de la Mercè in September often includes outdoor performances and activities in parks around the city.

1. **Pace Yourself**: Don't try to pack too much into each day. Leave time for spontaneous exploration, rest, and simply enjoying the outdoor spaces. Sometimes the unplanned moments become the most memorable.

1. **Mix Active and Relaxed Activities**: Balance high-energy activities like the treetop adventure course with more relaxed experiences like a picnic in Laberint d'Horta. This helps prevent exhaustion and keeps the itinerary enjoyable for all family members.

1. **Local Transportation**: Consider using Barcelona's efficient public transportation system to reach some of the outdoor destinations. It can be an adventure in itself and reduces the stress of navigating an unfamiliar city by car.

1. **Dining Flexibility**: While we've suggested some dining options, be flexible. Pack snacks for impromptu picnics, or be open to trying local cafes you discover during your adventures. Sometimes the unplanned meals become the most memorable.

Remember, the goal of your outdoor adventure in Barcelona is not just to see everything, but to experience the city's natural beauty and create lasting family memories. Don't be afraid to go off-script if you discover something that particularly interests your family. The best adventures often come from spontaneous decisions and unexpected discoveries!

CHAPTER SIX - Creativity and The Arts

Itinerary Overview

Barcelona, a city pulsing with creativity, offers families an unparalleled opportunity to immerse themselves in the world of art and imagination. This adventure will take you on a journey through the city's vibrant artistic landscape, from interactive museums to hands-on workshops, and from street performances to awe-inspiring architecture.

For a half-day adventure, start your morning at the whimsical MIBA (Museu d'Idees i Invents de Barcelona), where creativity knows no bounds. Follow this with a stroll down La Rambla to witness the city's living statues and street performers, then cap off your artistic exploration with a visit to the Centre d'Artesania Catalunya for a hands-on craft workshop.

If you have a full day to dedicate to creativity, begin at the MIBA, then make your way to the Barcelona Museum of Contemporary Art (MACBA) for a dose of modern artistic expression. After lunch, engage in a family- friendly graffiti workshop in the vibrant El Raval neighborhood. As the day winds down, take in a mesmerizing performance at the Gran Teatre del Liceu, Barcelona's grand opera house.

These itineraries are designed to spark creativity and foster a love for the arts in children of all ages. Remember, Barcelona's artistic spirit is everywhere – in its architecture, street art, and even in the way locals express themselves. Keep your eyes and hearts open to the beauty and inspiration that surrounds you in this magical city.

Detailed Activities and Experiences

MIBA (Museu d'Idees i Invents de Barcelona)

Step into a world where imagination reigns supreme at the MIBA, a unique museum dedicated to ideas and inventions. This playful space is perfect for families with children of all ages, as it encourages visitors to think outside the box and dream up their own inventions.

As you explore the museum's colorful exhibits, you'll encounter a variety of quirky inventions and innovative ideas. From a machine that makes square bubbles to a chair that gives hugs, each display is designed to spark creativity and inspire young minds. Interactive areas allow children to experiment with different materials and concepts, fostering their problem- solving skills and inventive spirit.

One of the highlights of the MIBA is the "Idea Workshop," where families can work together to create their own inventions. Under the guidance of friendly staff, you'll have access to various materials and tools to bring your ideas to life. Whether it's a new gadget to solve a everyday problem or a fantastical machine from your imagination, the process of creating together will be a memorable experience for the whole family.

Contact Information:

- Address: Carrer de la Ciutat, 7, 08002 Barcelona, Spain

- Phone: +34 933 32 79 30
- Operating Hours: Tuesday to Friday: 10:00 AM - 2:00 PM, 4:00 PM - 7:00 PM; Saturday and Sunday: 11:00 AM - 8:00 PM; Closed on Mondays

Street Art and Living Statues on La Rambla

La Rambla, Barcelona's most famous street, is a living, breathing work of art. This bustling pedestrian thoroughfare is home to an ever-changing array of street performers and living statues that will captivate children and adults alike.

As you stroll down La Rambla, you'll encounter a diverse cast of characters frozen in time. From historical figures to fantastical creatures, these living statues come to life with the clink of a coin, delighting onlookers with their sudden movements and interactions. Encourage your children to choose their favorite statues and try to guess what they might do when they move. It's a great opportunity to discuss different art forms and the skill required to remain perfectly still for long periods.

Interspersed among the living statues, you'll find a variety of street performers showcasing their talents. From acrobats and jugglers to musicians and magicians, there's always something happening on La Rambla. Take time to watch these performances together, discussing the different skills on display and perhaps even trying out some simple tricks or dance moves yourselves when you get back to your hotel.

As you explore, keep an eye out for the colorful mosaic by Joan Miró embedded in the pavement near the Liceu Theater. This is a great opportunity to introduce children to the concept of public art and how it can transform everyday spaces into something magical.

Thank you for making it this far!

I greatly appreciate the time you took to give my book a read,as a small indie publisher it means a lot and I hope that I am making a difference for you visit to Barcelona.

If you have G0 seconds your honest feedback on Amazon would mean the world to me., it does wonders for the book and I love hearing about your experience with it.

To Leave Your Feedback

1. Open your camera App
2. Point your mobile device at the QR code below
3. The review page will appear in your web browser

Or

You can click this link:https://www.amazon.com/dp/[1]
B0DK2LV8GX

---

1. http://www.amazon.com/dp/

Contact Information:

   - Location: La Rambla, Barcelona, Spain

- Note: Street performers and living statues can be found along the entire length of La Rambla, but are most concentrated in the central and southern sections.
- Best times to visit: Late morning to early evening, when the street is bustling with activity.

Centre d'Artesania Catalunya

Tucked away in the Gothic Quarter, the Centre d'Artesania Catalunya offers a unique opportunity for families to dive into the world of traditional Catalan crafts. This center is not just a showcase of beautiful handmade items, but also a place where you can learn about and participate in various craft-making processes.

Upon entering, you'll be greeted by an array of exquisite handcrafted items, from ceramics and textiles to glassware and jewelry. Take time to explore the exhibits with your children, discussing the different techniques used to create each piece. The center often has artisans working on-site, providing a chance to see master craftspeople in action and ask questions about their processes.

The highlight for families is the range of workshops offered at the center. These hands-on sessions are designed to introduce participants to various traditional Catalan crafts. Depending on the day and season, you might find yourself learning the basics of ceramic painting, trying your hand at weaving, or creating a simple piece of jewelry. These workshops are an excellent way for children to develop fine motor skills, learn about Catalan culture, and create a unique souvenir to take home.

Contact Information:

  - Address: Carrer dels Banys Nous, 11, 08002 Barcelona, Spain

- Phone: +34 934 G7 4G G0
- Operating Hours: Monday to Friday: 10:00 AM - 8:00 PM; Saturday:
10:00 AM - 2:00 PM and 4:00 PM - 8:00 PM; Closed on Sunday

90

Barcelona Museum of Contemporary Art (MACBA)

The Barcelona Museum of Contemporary Art, known locally as MACBA, is a treasure trove of modern and contemporary art that offers a unique experience for families. While contemporary art might seem challenging for younger visitors, MACBA goes out of its way to make art accessible and engaging for all ages.

As you approach the museum, take a moment to appreciate its striking architecture. The gleaming white building, designed by American architect Richard Meier, is a work of art in itself. Encourage your children to describe what they see and how the building makes them feel – this is a great way to start thinking about how art can evoke emotions.

Inside, you'll find a diverse collection of art from the mid-20th century to the present day. The museum's family programs are particularly noteworthy. On weekends and during school holidays, MACBA offers specially designed tours and workshops for families. These activities are tailored to different age groups and often involve interactive elements that help children engage with the art on display.

One of the highlights for families is the "MACBA in Family" program, which includes guided visits and hands-on art-making activities inspired by the museum's collection. These sessions are a fantastic way for children to learn about different artistic styles and techniques, and to express their own creativity in response to what they've seen.

Contact Information:

- Address: Plaça dels Àngels, 1, 08001 Barcelona, Spain

- Phone: +34 934 12 08 10

- Operating Hours: Monday, Wednesday, Thursday, and Friday: 11:00 AM

- 7:30 PM; Saturday: 10:00 AM - 8:00 PM; Sunday and public holidays: 10:00 AM - 3:00 PM; Closed on Tuesdays (except public holidays)

- Note: Check the website for the schedule of family programs and workshops.

El Raval, one of Barcelona's most diverse and creative neighborhoods, is home to a thriving street art scene. For families looking to explore this vibrant form of urban expression, a guided graffiti workshop offers an exciting and hands-on experience.

These workshops, led by local street artists, begin with a short walking tour of El Raval's most impressive murals and graffiti pieces. As you explore, your guide will explain the history of street art in Barcelona, the techniques used by different artists, and the messages behind some of the works. This is a great opportunity for children to learn about how art can be used to express ideas and transform public spaces.

After the tour, it's time to get creative! In a safe, designated area, families will have the chance to try their hand at graffiti art. Don't worry – all materials provided are child-friendly and washable. Under the guidance of your instructor, you'll learn basic spray painting techniques and work together to create your own colorful masterpiece.

This workshop not only allows children to express their creativity in a new medium but also opens up discussions about public art, urban culture, and the responsible use of public spaces. It's a unique way to engage with Barcelona's contemporary art scene and create lasting memories as a family.

Contact Information:

- Provider: Barcelona Street Style Tour
- Address: Workshop location in El Raval will be provided upon booking

- Phone: +34 GG5 82 02 G

- Operating Hours: Workshops are typically held on weekends and can be arranged for private groups on other days. Advance booking is required.

Gran Teatre del Liceu

No artistic adventure in Barcelona would be complete without a visit to the Gran Teatre del Liceu, one of Europe's greatest opera houses. While a full opera might be too long for younger children, the Liceu offers a range of family-friendly performances and activities that make this iconic venue accessible to all ages.

Before your visit, take some time to admire the theater's grand façade on La Rambla. The building itself is a testament to Barcelona's love affair with the arts, having been rebuilt and restored multiple times since its opening in 1847. As you enter the opulent lobby, encourage your children to imagine the grand balls and performances that have taken place here over the centuries.

The Liceu's "Petit Liceu" program is specifically designed for young audiences. These shortened, adapted versions of classic operas and ballets are perfect for introducing children to the world of performing arts. With colorful costumes, engaging storytelling, and interactive elements, these performances capture the imagination of young viewers while maintaining the essence of the original works.

In addition to performances, the Liceu offers guided tours that are suitable for families. These tours take you behind the scenes, allowing you to explore the grand auditorium, peek into the orchestra pit, and learn about the intricate workings of a major opera house. It's a fascinating glimpse into a world that most people never get to see.

Contact Information:

- Address: La Rambla, 51-59, 08002 Barcelona, Spain

- Phone: +34 934 85 99 00
- Operating Hours for Tours: Monday to Friday: 9:30 AM - 3:30 PM (last tour at 2:30 PM); Saturday: 9:30 AM - 1:30 PM (last tour at 12:30 PM); Closed on Sundays
- Note: Performance schedules vary. Check the website for upcoming "Petit Liceu" shows and book in advance.

Recommendations for Useful Tools

1. **Barcelona Culture App**: This official app from the Barcelona City Council is a comprehensive guide to the city's cultural offerings. It provides up-to-date information on exhibitions, performances, and events across the city, many of which are family-friendly. The app also includes a section dedicated to activities for children and young people.

- Available for iOS and Android

1. **ARTiPLAY**: This innovative app turns Barcelona into a giant, interactive canvas. Using augmented reality technology, it allows users to discover hidden digital artworks throughout the city. As you explore Barcelona, your phone becomes a window into a world of virtual sculptures and paintings, making your artistic adventure feel like a citywide treasure hunt.

1. **BarcelonaMuseums.com**: This website is an excellent resource for planning your artistic adventures in Barcelona. It provides detailed information about all of the city's museums, including those specializing in art and creativity. The site offers suggestions for family-friendly exhibits and activities, making it easier to tailor your visits to your children's interests and ages.

1. **Street Art Barcelona Map**: For families interested in exploring Barcelona's vibrant street art scene, this online map is an invaluable tool. It pinpoints the locations of notable murals and graffiti pieces throughout the city, complete with photos and information about the artists. Use it to create your own self-guided street art tour.

1. **TimeOut Barcelona**: While not exclusively focused on art and creativity, TimeOut Barcelona's website and app are excellent resources for finding current exhibitions, performances, and family-friendly events. Their "Things to Do" section often features unique creative experiences that might not be found in traditional guidebooks.

Remember to download these apps and bookmark these websites before your trip. They'll help you stay informed about the latest artistic happenings in Barcelona and may introduce you to creative experiences you might otherwise miss!

Family-friendly Dining Recommendations

La Foodieteca

Located in the heart of the artistic El Born neighborhood, La Foodieteca is more than just a restaurant – it's a culinary canvas where food meets art.

This unique eatery offers a playful and creative dining experience that will delight both children and adults.

The interior of La Foodieteca is a feast for the eyes, with colorful murals, quirky sculptures, and ever-changing art installations. The menu is equally creative, featuring dishes that are as visually stunning as they are delicious. Children will love the "Paint Your Own Pizza" option, where they're given a plain pizza base and a variety of colorful vegetable "paints" to create their own edible masterpiece.

For the adults, the menu offers a range of innovative tapas and main courses that blend traditional Catalan flavors with modern culinary techniques.

Don't miss their signature "Deconstructed Paella," a playful take on the classic Spanish dish.

Throughout the meal, keep an eye out for the restaurant's roving artists. These performers move from table to table, creating quick sketches, performing magic tricks, or even composing impromptu poems inspired by the diners. It's an immersive experience that perfectly complements your day of artistic exploration in Barcelona.

Contact Information:

- Address: Carrer dels Flassaders, 30, 08003 Barcelona, Spain

- Phone: +34 933 10 21 80
- Operating Hours: Tuesday to Sunday: 1:00 PM - 4:00 PM and 7:00 PM - 11:00 PM; Closed on Mondays

- Note: Reservations are recommended, especially for dinner

El Jardí de l'Ópera

Nestled within the iconic Liceu Opera House, El Jardí de l'Ópera offers a unique dining experience that combines culinary artistry with theatrical flair. This restaurant is perfect for families looking to extend their artistic adventure into mealtime.

The restaurant's outdoor terrace, set in a beautiful garden courtyard, feels like a secret oasis in the heart of the bustling city. Inside, the decor pays homage to the building's operatic heritage, with vintage posters, ornate mirrors, and plush velvet seating.

The menu at El Jardí de l'Ópera is a celebration of Catalan cuisine with a creative twist. For children, they offer a special "Little Maestro's Menu" featuring dishes inspired by famous operas. Adults can enjoy a range of sophisticated dishes that change seasonally, always emphasizing local, fresh ingredients.

What makes dining here truly special is the occasional pop-up performances by opera singers and musicians from the Liceu. These short, family-friendly performances bring a touch of operatic magic to your meal without overwhelming younger diners.

97

CHAPTER SEVEN - The Foodie Family

Welcome to a mouthwatering journey through Barcelona's vibrant culinary scene! This chapter is designed to guide families with children aged 3-15 through the city's delectable delights, offering unique food experiences that will tantalize your taste buds and create lasting memories. Get ready to embark on a gastronomic adventure that will introduce you to the flavors, aromas, and traditions that make Barcelona a food lover's paradise.

Itinerary Overview

Half-Day Plan (4-5 hours):

1. Start your day with a visit to the colorful Santa Caterina Market
2. Participate in a kid-friendly paella cooking class
3. Enjoy your homemade paella lunch
4. Indulge in artisanal ice cream at Gelaaati di Marco

Full-Day Plan (8-9 hours):

1. Begin with a family-friendly food tour in the Gothic Quarter
2. Explore the Santa Caterina Market
3. Attend a chocolate-making workshop
4. Have lunch at a traditional Catalan restaurant
5. Participate in a kid-friendly paella cooking class

G. Enjoy your homemade paella dinner

7. End the day with artisanal ice cream at Gelaaati di Marco

These itineraries are designed to immerse your family in Barcelona's rich culinary heritage while keeping things fun and engaging for children of all ages. From hands-on cooking experiences to guided food tours and market visits, you'll discover the flavors that make this city so special. Remember, these plans are flexible – feel free to adjust them based on your family's preferences and energy levels!

Detailed Activities and Experiences

1. Family-Friendly Food Tour in the Gothic Quarter

Start your culinary adventure with a guided food tour through the enchanting Gothic Quarter. This experience is perfect for introducing your family to the diverse flavors of Catalan cuisine while exploring the historic heart of Barcelona.

Your knowledgeable guide will lead you through winding medieval streets, stopping at various family-owned establishments to sample local delicacies. Children will love the interactive nature of the tour, as they get to taste different foods and learn about their history and cultural significance. Some highlights might include trying freshly baked bread from a centuries-old bakery, sampling artisanal cheeses, and tasting traditional Catalan sausages.

The tour is designed to be engaging for all ages, with the guide incorporating fun facts and stories that will captivate both children and adults. They might share tales of ancient Roman ruins hidden beneath the city or point out architectural details that bring Barcelona's rich history to life. This experience not only satisfies your taste buds but also provides a delightful blend of culinary education and historical exploration.

99

Contact Information:

* Barcelona Taste Food Tours
* Phone: +34 931 81G 28G
* Address: Tours usually start in Plaça Reial, Gothic Quarter
* Operating Hours: Tours typically run daily at 10:30 AM and 4:30 PM

2. Santa Caterina Market Visit

No foodie adventure in Barcelona would be complete without exploring one of its vibrant markets. The Santa Caterina Market, with its stunning undulating roof of colorful ceramic tiles, offers a feast for both the eyes and the palate. This market is less touristy than the famous La Boqueria, providing a more authentic local experience.

As you enter, you'll be greeted by a kaleidoscope of colors, aromas, and sounds. The market is home to numerous stalls selling fresh produce, meats, cheeses, fish, and local specialties. Engage your children by turning the visit into a scavenger hunt – challenge them to find the most unusual fruit or vegetable, count how many types of olives they can spot, or identify different fish at the seafood stalls.

Many vendors offer free samples, so encourage your little ones to taste new flavors. They might discover a love for manchego cheese, olives, or perhaps even a slice of jamón ibérico. For a fun activity, give each family member a small budget and task them with selecting ingredients for a picnic lunch.

This not only teaches children about local foods but also helps them practice basic math and decision-making skills.

Before leaving, stop by one of the market's small eateries for a quick snack or refreshment. The market's lively atmosphere and array of culinary treasures make it an excellent place to immerse your family in Barcelona's food culture

Contact Information:

* Santa Caterina Market
* Phone: +34 933 195 740
* Address: Av. de Francesc Cambó, 1G, 08003 Barcelona

* Operating Hours: Monday 7:30 AM - 3:00 PM, Tuesday to Friday 7:30 AM - 8:30 PM, Saturday 7:30 AM - 3:30 PM, Closed on Sundays

* Reservations: Not required for general visits

3. Chocolate-Making Workshop

Delight your family's sweet tooth with a hands-on chocolate-making workshop at one of Barcelona's artisanal chocolatiers. This activity combines history, science, and of course, plenty of delicious tasting opportunities!

The workshop begins with a brief introduction to the history of chocolate, including its origins in Central America and its journey to Europe.

Children will be fascinated to learn that chocolate was once considered a precious commodity, sometimes used as currency! The chocolatier will then explain the process of transforming cacao beans into the chocolate we know and love today.

Next comes the fun part – making your own chocolates! Under the guidance of expert chocolatiers, your family will learn to temper chocolate, create molded shapes, and even design your own chocolate bars. Children will love getting their hands messy as they experiment with different flavors and decorations. They can create personalized chocolate gifts for friends back home or design a special treat for themselves.

101

Throughout the workshop, you'll have the opportunity to taste various types of chocolate, from rich dark varieties to creamy milk chocolates. The chocolatier will teach you how to properly taste chocolate, engaging all your senses in the process. This workshop not only satisfies your sweet cravings but also provides a fun, educational experience that the whole family can enjoy together

Contact Information:

* Chök - The Chocolate Kitchen
* Phone: +34 933 042 3G0
* Address: Carrer del Carme, 3, 08001 Barcelona

* Operating Hours: Workshops typically run on weekends at 11:00 AM and 4:00 PM

4. Kid-Friendly Paella Cooking Class

Immerse your family in Spanish culinary tradition with a hands-on paella cooking class. This iconic dish is not only delicious but also fun to prepare, making it perfect for a family activity. The class is designed to be engaging for all ages, with tasks suitable for both little helpers and budding teen chefs.

Your experience begins with a brief introduction to paella's history and its significance in Spanish cuisine. The chef will explain the key ingredients and their roles in creating the perfect paella. Children will be fascinated to learn about saffron, the world's most expensive spice, which gives paella its distinctive yellow color and unique flavor.

Younger children might help wash and sort vegetables or measure out ingredients, while older kids can assist with chopping and stirring. The chef will guide you through each step, from sautéing the sofrito (a flavor base of vegetables and spices) to adding the rice and stock, and finally, arranging the seafood or meat on top.

While the paella simmers, filling the kitchen with mouthwatering aromas, the chef might teach you how to prepare a simple Spanish appetizer or dessert.

This could be anything from pan con tomate (bread rubbed with tomato and garlic) to crema catalana (similar to crème brûlée).

The best part, of course, is sitting down together to enjoy the fruits of your labor. As you savor your homemade paella, you'll not only be treating your taste buds but also creating lasting family memories. This hands-on experience provides a deeper appreciation for Spanish cuisine and gives your children valuable cooking skills they can use for years to come.

Contact Information:

* Barcelona Cooking
* Phone: +34 934 87G 217
* Address: La Rambla, 58, 08002 Barcelona
* Operating Hours: Classes typically run daily at 10:00 AM and 5:00 PM
* Reservations: Required, book online or by phone

5. Artisanal Ice Cream at Gelaaati di Marco

After a day of culinary adventures, treat your family to some of the best ice cream in Barcelona at Gelaaati di Marco. This charming gelateria offers a perfect sweet ending to your foodie journey, with its array of unique and classic flavors crafted from high-quality, natural ingredients.

As you enter the shop, you'll be greeted by a colorful display of gelato in various enticing hues and textures. The friendly staff is always happy to offer tastings, so don't hesitate to try a few flavors before making your final decision. Encourage your children to be adventurous – they might discover a new favorite!

103

What sets Gelaaati di Marco apart is its commitment to using fresh, seasonal ingredients and creating innovative flavor combinations. You might find traditional favorites like chocolate and vanilla alongside more unusual options such as basil, saffron, or even olive oil gelato. For fruit lovers, there's a rainbow of sorbets made with ripe, juicy fruits.

While enjoying your gelato, take a moment to appreciate the artistry that goes into each scoop. The gelato here is crafted daily in small batches, ensuring the highest quality and freshest taste. It's a great opportunity to discuss with your children the difference between mass-produced ice cream and artisanal gelato, touching on topics like ingredient quality and traditional production methods.

For a fun family activity, why not have each family member choose a different flavor and then share tastes? You can discuss the various flavor profiles and vote on your favorites. It's a delicious way to expand your palate and create sweet memories together.

Contact Information:

* Gelaaati di Marco
* Phone: +34 933 042 29G
* Address: Carrer de la Llibreteria, 7, 08002 Barcelona

* Operating Hours: Daily from 11:00 AM to 11:00 PM (May extend to midnight in summer)

* Reservations: Not required

Recommendations for Useful Tools

To enhance your culinary adventure in Barcelona, consider using these helpful apps and resources:

1. **Eat With Locals App:** This app connects you with local hosts offering authentic home-cooked meals. It's a great way to experience traditional Catalan cuisine in a family setting.

1. **Google Translate:** An essential tool for deciphering menus and communicating dietary requirements. The camera feature can instantly translate text, making it easier to navigate markets and restaurants.

1. **Fork:** A restaurant booking app that's widely used in Barcelona. It often offers special discounts and allows you to filter for family-friendly venues.

1. **Barcelona Foodie Guide:** This app provides curated lists of restaurants, cafes, and food experiences, complete with user reviews and photos.

1. **Time Out Barcelona:** Offers up-to-date information on food events, markets, and new restaurant openings in the city.

Remember to download these apps and any necessary offline content before your trip to avoid using excessive data or relying on potentially spotty Wi-Fi connections.

Tips for Families with Dietary Restrictions

Navigating dietary restrictions while traveling can be challenging, but Barcelona is increasingly accommodating to various dietary needs. Here are some tips to ensure everyone in your family can enjoy the local cuisine:

1. **Learn key phrases:** Familiarize yourself with Spanish phrases related to your dietary restrictions. For example, "Soy alérgico/a a..." means "I'm allergic to..." and "Sin gluten" means "gluten-free."

1. **Communicate clearly:** Don't hesitate to ask about ingredients or preparation methods. Most restaurants are happy to accommodate if they understand your needs.

1. **Research in advance:** Look up restaurants that cater to your specific dietary requirements. Barcelona has a growing number of vegetarian, vegan, and gluten-free friendly establishments.

1. **Pack snacks:** Bring along some safe snacks for picky eaters or those with severe allergies, just in case you can't find suitable options while out exploring.

1. **Visit markets:** Fresh produce markets are great for finding allergen-free foods and ingredients if you're self-catering.

G. **Consider apartment rentals:** Having access to a kitchen allows you to prepare safe meals for family members with strict dietary needs.

1. **Be flexible:** Encourage children to try new foods within their dietary restrictions. They might discover new favorites!

1. **Plan ahead for restaurants:** Call ahead or email restaurants to discuss your dietary needs, especially for more severe allergies or restrictions.

Remember, many traditional Spanish dishes are naturally suited to various diets. For example, gazpacho is vegan, while many tapas are gluten-free.

With a little preparation and communication, your family can safely enjoy Barcelona's culinary delights.

Family-Friendly Dining Recommendations

Barcelona offers a wealth of family-friendly dining options that showcase local cuisine while catering to younger palates. Here are some unique recommendations not mentioned in other chapters:

1. **El Nacional** - This multi-space culinary complex houses four restaurants and four specialized bars under one stunning roof. The variety ensures there's something for everyone, from fresh seafood to juicy steaks.

* Address: Passeig de Gràcia, 24 Bis, 08007 Barcelona
* Phone: +34 935 18 50 53

* Hours: Sunday to Thursday 12:00 PM - 1:00 AM, Friday and Saturday 12:00 PM - 2:00 AM

2. **Aguaribay** - A charming vegetarian and vegan restaurant that proves healthy eating can be delicious and fun. They offer creative plant-based versions of traditional Catalan dishes.

* Address: Carrer del Taulat, 95, 08005 Barcelona
* Phone: +34 933 09 57 G1

* Hours: Tuesday to Saturday 1:00 PM - 4:00 PM and 8:00 PM - 11:00 PM, Closed Sunday and Monday

3. **La Boqueria Food Market** - While the market itself was mentioned in a previous chapter, we recommend trying the sit-down eateries inside for a unique dining experience. El Quim de la Boqueria is especially family- friendly.

* Address: La Rambla, 91, 08001 Barcelona
* Phone: +34 933 18 25 84 (El Quim de la Boqueria)
* Hours: Monday to Saturday 8:00 AM - 8:30 PM, Closed on Sundays

Must-try dishes at these locations include:

- The seafood paella at El Nacional
- Vegan "butifarra" (Catalan sausage) at Aguaribay

- Fresh fruit juices and "huevos estrellados" (fried eggs over potatoes) at El Quim in
  La Boqueria

- The "Alice in Wonderland" themed pancakes at Pudding
- Grilled sardines or calamari at La Paradeta

Remember to make reservations when possible, especially for dinner, as popular restaurants can get quite busy. Many of these establishments offer children's menus or smaller portions for younger diners – don't hesitate to ask!

Creative Memory Makers

Enhance your family's culinary adventure in Barcelona with these unique and engaging activities that will create lasting memories:

1. **Barcelona Food Scavenger Hunt:** Create a list of traditional Catalan ingredients or dishes for your family to find and try throughout your trip. Include items like pa amb tomàquet (bread with tomato), crema catalana, or fideuà. Award points for each item found and tasted, with bonus points for learning how to pronounce them correctly in Catalan!

1. **Family Food Photography Challenge:** Encourage each family member to take photos of their favorite dishes, market finds, or culinary experiences. At the end of each day, have a "show and tell" session where everyone shares their best food photo and explains why they chose it. You could even create a digital family cookbook with the photos and recipes you've discovered.

1. **Create Your Own Tapas:** After learning about various Spanish tapas, challenge each family member to invent their own unique tapa using local ingredients. You could prepare these in your accommodation if you have kitchen access, or simply draw and describe your creations. Vote on the most creative or delicious-sounding invention!

1. **Barcelona Food Diary:** Provide each family member with a small notebook to use as a food diary. Encourage them to write or draw about new foods they've tried, interesting ingredients they've discovered, or memorable meals. They can include details like taste, texture, and even how the food made them feel. This becomes a personalized souvenir of your culinary journey.

G. **Foodie Family Talent Show:** Inspired by cooking shows, host a family talent show where each member demonstrates a culinary skill they've learned during the trip. This could be anything from properly cutting jamón to making the perfect paella. Film these "performances" to create a fun family video keepsake.

1. **Market Sketch Session:** Bring along some colored pencils and paper, and spend time at one of Barcelona's beautiful markets sketching the vibrant produce, meats, or seafood on display. This encourages careful observation and appreciation of the local food culture. You could compile these sketches into a family art book about Barcelona's markets.

1. **Aroma Memory Game:** Collect small samples of aromatic ingredients common in Catalan cooking (like saffron, rosemary, or orange zest). Create a game where family members try to

identify the scents while blindfolded. This activity engages the senses and helps create strong olfactory memories of your trip.

Tips for Customizing the Itinerary

Every family is unique, so feel free to adapt this foodie adventure to suit your specific interests and needs. Here are some tips to help you customize your culinary journey through Barcelona:

1. **Consider your children's ages:** Younger children might enjoy more hands-on activities like the chocolate workshop, while teenagers might appreciate the historical context provided in food tours. Adjust the itinerary to match your children's attention spans and interests.

1. **Balance food activities with other sightseeing:** While this chapter focuses on culinary experiences, remember to intersperse these with visits to Barcelona's other attractions. For example, you could visit the Santa Caterina Market in the morning, then explore the nearby Barcelona Cathedral before your afternoon cooking class.

1. **Adjust for food preferences:** If your family has strong likes or dislikes, feel free to swap out suggested restaurants or food stops for ones that better match your tastes. Barcelona has a diverse food scene that can accommodate various preferences.

1. **Consider your energy levels:** Food tours and cooking classes can be quite involved. If you need a more relaxed day, consider spreading activities out over multiple days or replacing a hands-on activity with a visit to a food museum like the Chocolate Museum.

1. **Incorporate seasonal events:** Check if there are any food festivals or seasonal markets happening during your visit. These can be great additions to your itinerary and offer unique local experiences.

G. **Plan around mealtimes:** Remember that Barcelona typically eats later than many other countries. Lunch is usually around 2:00 PM and dinner rarely starts before 8:00 PM. Plan your activities accordingly, and don't forget to include time for the Spanish tradition of "merienda" (afternoon snack) around 5:00 PM.

1. **Include downtime:** Food experiences can be quite rich and intense. Make sure to include some downtime in your schedule for rest or free exploration. This could be as simple as enjoying a leisurely picnic in a park with foods you've collected during your market visit.

1. **Consider food souvenirs:** If you want to bring a taste of Barcelona home, allocate some time for shopping for non-perishable food souvenirs. Items like saffron, smoked paprika, or high-quality olive oil make great mementos of your trip.

110

1. **Include downtime:** Food experiences can be quite rich and intense. Make sure to include some downtime in your schedule for rest or free exploration. This could be as simple as enjoying a leisurely picnic in a park with foods you've collected during your market visit.

1. **Consider food souvenirs:** If you want to bring a taste of Barcelona home, allocate some time for shopping for non-perishable food souvenirs. Items like saffron, smoked paprika, or high-quality olive oil make great mementos of your trip.

1. **Embrace spontaneity:** While it's good to have a plan, some of the best food discoveries happen by chance. Leave some flexibility in your schedule to explore an interesting-looking café or follow the aroma of freshly baked bread down a side street.

1. **Engage your children in planning:** Let each family member choose an activity or restaurant they're most excited about. This gives children a sense of ownership over the trip and ensures everyone has something to look forward to.

Remember, the goal is to create a memorable family experience that introduces you to Barcelona's rich culinary heritage. Don't feel pressured to do everything – it's often better to do fewer activities more thoroughly and enjoyably than to rush through a packed itinerary.

By following these tips and customizing the suggested itinerary, you can create a food adventure that perfectly suits your family's tastes, energy levels, and interests. Whether you're sampling tapas, learning to make paella, or exploring vibrant markets, you're sure to come away with a deeper appreciation for Barcelona's fantastic food culture and a treasure trove of delicious family memories.

CHAPTER EIGHT - The Science & Education Trail

Welcome, curious families, to an exhilarating journey through Barcelona's lesser-known scientific wonders! This chapter will guide you through a day filled with unique discoveries, hands-on learning, and exciting experiments. Get ready to explore hidden gems, cutting-edge research facilities, and interactive workshops that will ignite your children's passion for science and discovery.

Itinerary Overview

Half-Day Plan (4-5 hours):

1. Start your morning at the Barcelona Biomedical Research Park
2. Enjoy lunch at the Hydrogen Bar
3. Explore the Glòries Tower and its surrounding technological hub

Full-Day Plan (8-9 hours):

1. Begin at the Barcelona Biomedical Research Park
2. Lunch at the Hydrogen Bar
3. Visit the Glòries Tower and technological hub
4. Explore the Ciutadella Park's scientific institutions
5. End your day with dinner at the Galactic Cantina

112

Detailed Activities and Experiences Barcelona Biomedical Research Park (PRBB)

The Barcelona Biomedical Research Park (PRBB) is one of the largest biomedical research hubs in southern Europe. While it's primarily a working research facility, they offer fascinating guided tours that provide a glimpse into the world of cutting-edge biomedical science.

Start your visit with the "Windows to Science" tour, specially designed for families. This tour takes you through various laboratories and research areas, with interactive stops along the way. Your children will be amazed to see real scientists at work, using advanced microscopes and other high-tech equipment.

One of the highlights is the zebrafish facility, where researchers study these tiny fish to understand human diseases. The guide will explain how zebrafish share 70% of their genes with humans, making them excellent models for studying genetics and developing new treatments.

Next, visit the bioinformatics department, where powerful computers analyze vast amounts of biological data. Here, your family can participate in a simplified data analysis activity, giving you a taste of how scientists use technology to understand complex biological systems.

The tour also includes a stop at the genomics lab, where you'll learn about DNA sequencing and its importance in personalized medicine. Children will have the opportunity to extract DNA from a banana in a fun, hands-on experiment they can take home.

End your visit with a Q&A session with a young researcher, inspiring your children with stories of real-world scientific discoveries and career paths in biomedical science.

Contact Information:

- Address: Carrer del Dr. Aiguader, 88, 08003 Barcelona, Spain

- Phone: +34 933 1G 00 00
- Hours: Guided tours available Monday to Friday, 10:00 AM and 3:00 PM (reservation required)

Glòries Tower and Technological Hub

The newly renovated Glòries area has become Barcelona's technological and innovation district. At its heart stands the iconic Glòries Tower (formerly known as Agbar Tower), surrounded by a cluster of tech companies and start-ups.

Begin your visit at the Glòries Tower Visitor Center. Although the tower itself is occupied by offices, the visitor center offers an engaging exhibition on sustainable urban technology. Interactive displays showcase Barcelona's smart city initiatives, from intelligent traffic management to energy- efficient buildings.

Next, take a stroll through the surrounding tech hub. Many companies in the area have street-level windows where you can observe engineers and designers at work. Look out for the "Innovation Window" signs, which indicate spots where companies showcase their latest projects to the public.

Don't miss the outdoor "Tech Playground" adjacent to the tower. This unique park features swings that generate electricity as you play, solar- powered charging stations for devices, and an augmented reality sandbox where children can shape topography and watch as the projection adapts in real-time.

For a hands-on experience, visit the "Maker Space" workshop. Here, families can participate in short, guided projects using 3D printers, simple robotics kits, and other modern maker tools. Sessions are offered hourly and are suitable for children aged 8 and up (younger children can participate with close parental supervision).

Finish your visit at the "Future Barcelona" exhibit, where you can use VR headsets to explore how technology might shape the city in the coming decades. This is a great opportunity to discuss with your children how science and technology can address urban challenges and improve quality of life.

Contact Information:

- Address: Plaça de les Glòries Catalanes, 08018 Barcelona, Spain

- Phone: +34 932 54 00 00
- Hours: Visitor Center and outdoor areas open daily 9:00 AM - 8:00 PM, Maker Space workshops 10:00 AM - G:00 PM (reservation recommended)

Ciutadella Park's Scientific Institutions

Ciutadella Park is not just a beautiful green space; it's also home to several scientific institutions that offer unique learning experiences for families.

Start at the Barcelona Zoo's Research and Conservation Center. While separate from the main zoo, this facility offers weekly "Junior Scientist" workshops where children can learn about wildlife biology, conservation efforts, and animal behavior. Activities might include analyzing animal tracks, studying biodiversity, or learning about endangered species protection programs.

Next, visit the Martorell Museum of Geology, located within the park. This often-overlooked gem houses an impressive collection of minerals, fossils, and rocks. The museum offers a "Geology Detective" program for families, where children receive a special guidebook and must solve geological puzzles as they explore the exhibits. Don't miss the fluorescent mineral room, where ultraviolet light reveals the hidden colors of seemingly ordinary rocks.

Adjacent to the geology museum is the Castell dels Tres Dragons, which houses the Laboratory of Nature. Although not usually open to the public, they offer monthly "Open Lab Days" where families can tour the research facilities, participate in biodiversity workshops, and even help scientists sort and catalog specimens.

End your park science tour at the Hivernacle, a beautiful 19th-century greenhouse. Recently repurposed as an urban agriculture research center, it now offers tours and workshops on sustainable farming techniques, vertical gardening, and the science of plant growth. Children can participate in planting activities and take home their own mini hydroponic system.

Contact Information:

- Barcelona Zoo Research Center
- Address: Parc de la Ciutadella, 08003 Barcelona, Spain

- Phone: +34 932 25 G7 80
- Hours: Junior Scientist workshops every Saturday, 10:00 AM - 12:00 PM (reservation required)

- Martorell Museum of Geology
- Address: Parc de la Ciutadella, 08003 Barcelona, Spain

- Phone: +34 932 5G 21 22

- Hours: Tuesday to Sunday, 10:00 AM - G:30 PM

- Laboratory of Nature (Castell dels Tres Dragons)
- Address: Passeig de Picasso, 5, 08003 Barcelona, Spain

- Phone: +34 932 5G 21 00
- Hours: Open Lab Days on the first Sunday of each month, 11:00 AM - 2:00 PM

- Hivernacle Urban Agriculture Center
- Address: Passeig de Picasso, 08003 Barcelona, Spain

- Phone: +34 932 5G 21 50
- Hours: Tours and workshops Wednesday to Sunday, 10:00 AM - 1:00 PM and 3:00 PM - G:00 PM

Recommendations for Useful Tools

To enhance your family's learning experience on this unique Science & Education Trail, consider using these educational apps and tools:

1. **iNaturalist (iOS/Android)**: This citizen science app is perfect for your visit to Ciutadella Park. Use it to identify plants and animals, contributing to real scientific research as you explore.

1. **Nanoreisen (iOS/Android)**: Before your visit to the Barcelona Biomedical Research Park, use this app to take a virtual journey into the nanoworld of cells and molecules. It's a great way to prepare children for the concepts they'll encounter.

1. **Tinkercad (Web-based)**: This free, easy-to-use 3D modeling tool is excellent preparation for the Maker Space workshop at Glòries Tower. Practice at home, then see your designs come to life on a 3D printer.

1. **DIY.org (iOS/Android/Web)**: This app offers a wide range of science and technology challenges that kids can complete at home or while traveling. It's a great way to extend the learning from your Barcelona science adventure.
2. **Barcelona Science Scavenger Hunt (Custom Printable)**: We've created a downloadable scavenger hunt tailored to this Science & Education Trail. It includes clues and challenges related to each location, encouraging active engagement and keen observation.

Remember to download these apps and resources before your adventure to ensure you have them ready when you need them!

Family-friendly Dining Recommendations Hydrogen Bar

After your morning at the Barcelona Biomedical Research Park, head to the nearby Hydrogen Bar for a lunch that's equal parts delicious and educational. Despite its name, this isn't a place that serves drinks – it's a cutting-edge restaurant that uses molecular gastronomy techniques to create fascinating dishes.

The menu is designed to showcase scientific principles through food. Try the "Spherification Surprise," where your kids can watch as liquids are transformed into gel-like spheres right at your table. The "Nitrogen Ice Cream" dessert is always a hit, with servers using liquid nitrogen to instantly freeze and create custom ice cream flavors.

Don't miss the "Lab Hour" between 2-3 PM, where staff perform safe and entertaining food science demonstrations at your table. It's education disguised as mealtime entertainment!

Contact Information:

- Address: Carrer del Dr. Aiguader, 120, 08003 Barcelona, Spain

- Phone: +34 933 5G 10 00

- Hours: Monday to Saturday, 12:00 PM -

Galactic Cantina

For dinner, venture into the Galactic Cantina, a space-themed restaurant that combines astronomy education with dining. Located near the Fabra Observatory (but far enough to not overlap with other tour activities), this unique eatery takes you on a culinary journey through the cosmos.

The restaurant is designed to look like a space station, with "windows" that are actually screens showing real-time views from space telescopes. Each table is equipped with a tablet that provides information about the celestial objects you can see on the screens.

The menu features dishes inspired by space exploration and astronomical phenomena. Kids will love the "Mars Rover Rolls" (red-tinted bread rolls with a variety of fillings) and the "Nebula Nachos" (color-changing nachos that shift hues under special lights). For dessert, try the "Planetary Parfaits," layered treats that represent the structures of different planets in our solar system.

Throughout your meal, pop quizzes and fun facts about space appear on your table's tablet, turning dinner into an interactive learning experience. On clear nights, they even offer a short stargazing session on the rooftop after your meal.

Contact Information:

- Address: Carrer del Bosc, 33, 08017 Barcelona, Spain

- Phone: +34 934 17 5G 11

- Hours: Tuesday to Sunday, 7:00 PM - 11:00 PM (Closed on Mondays)

Creative Memory Makers

Make your Science & Education Trail adventure unforgettable with these unique, Barcelona-inspired activities:

1. **Biomedical Research Diary**: Inspired by your visit to the Barcelona Biomedical Research Park, create a family research diary. Each family member can choose a scientific question to investigate throughout your trip, recording observations and forming hypotheses.

1. **Barcelona Tech Time Capsule**: After exploring the Glòries tech hub, create a digital time capsule. Record video predictions about future technology and how it might change Barcelona. Save it to watch in 5 or 10 years!

1. **Ciutadella Park Biodiversity Challenge**: During your visit to Ciutadella Park, challenge each family member to safely photograph as many different species (plants, insects, birds) as they can. Use the iNaturalist app to identify them and contribute to citizen science projects.

1. **DIY Molecular Gastronomy**: Inspired by your meal at Hydrogen Bar, try some simple and safe molecular gastronomy experiments in your accommodation. Create fruit juice caviar or make instant ice cream using zip-lock bags and ice.

1. **Barcelona Skyline Silhouette**: After your visit to Glòries Tower, create a family art project depicting Barcelona's skyline. Use glow-in-the- dark paint to add constellations above the city, combining your urban and astronomical experiences.

G. **Science Busking Challenge**: Inspired by Barcelona's street performer tradition, challenge older kids to prepare a short "science busking" demonstration. They can perform simple, safe experiments for the family, explaining the science behind them.

7. **Barcelona Science Podcast**: Throughout your adventure, record short audio clips of your experiences, questions, and discoveries. At the end of the trip, edit them together into a family "podcast" episode about your Barcelona science adventure.

These activities will not only reinforce the scientific concepts you've encountered but also create lasting memories tied to your unique Barcelona experience.

Tips for Customizing the Itinerary

1. **Age-Appropriate Adjustments**:

- For families with younger children (3-7), focus more time on the hands- on activities at Ciutadella Park and the interactive exhibits at Glòries Tower.

- For older children and teens (8-15), allocate more time to the Barcelona Biomedical Research Park and consider scheduling a longer session at the Maker Space.

2. **Special Interests**:

- If your family is particularly interested in biology or medicine, extend your time at the Barcelona Biomedical Research Park and consider adding a visit to the Hospital de Sant Pau, which offers tours of its beautiful modernist buildings and insights into medical history.

- For tech enthusiasts, spend more time in the Glòries area and look into any special events or workshops happening at the numerous tech companies in the district.

121

3. **Seasonal Considerations**:

- Summer visitors should take advantage of the outdoor spaces in Ciutadella Park during the cooler morning hours.
- Winter visitors might want to focus more on indoor activities, spending more time at the Biomedical Research Park or the museums in Ciutadella Park.

4. **Mobility Needs**:

- If anyone in your group has mobility challenges, note that the Barcelona Biomedical Research Park and Glòries Tower area are fully accessible. Some parts of Ciutadella Park may be more challenging to navigate.

5. **Language Preferences**:

- While many exhibits offer information in multiple languages, consider requesting a guide who speaks your preferred language, especially for the more complex topics at the Biomedical Research Park.
G. **Budget Flexibility**:
- If you're looking to save money, focus on the free outdoor activities in Ciutadella Park and the public areas of the Glòries tech hub.
- For a splurge, look into private guided tours or exclusive workshops, like a longer session at the Maker Space or a more in-depth tour of the Biomedical Research Park.

7. **Time Management**:

- If you're short on time, prioritize the Biomedical Research Park tour and the Glòries Tower area, which offer the most unique experiences.
- With extra time, add more of the activities in Ciutadella Park or explore some of the tech company visitor centers around Glòries.

8. **Learning Styles**:

- For visual learners, focus on the exhibitions at Glòries Tower and the geological displays at the Martorell Museum.
- For hands-on learners, prioritize the Maker Space workshops and the activities at the Zoo Research Center.
- For auditory learners, make sure to attend guided tours and presentations at each location.

9. **Connecting to School Curriculum**:

- If possible, review your children's science curriculum before the trip. Look for ways to connect what they're learning in school to the real-world applications you'll see, especially at the Biomedical Research Park and the tech hub.

10. **Follow-Up Activities**:

- Consider ways to extend the learning experience after your trip. This could include science projects inspired by what you've seen, further research into topics that particularly interested your children, or even reaching out to some of the scientists or institutions you visited for more information.

11. **Local Events and Festivals**:

- Check if your visit coincides with any local science events or festivals. Barcelona often hosts events like the "Barcelona Ciència" festival or the "Researchers' Night" which could add exciting dimensions to your science adventure.

Remember, the goal is to create an engaging and memorable experience for your whole family. Don't be afraid to adjust the itinerary on the fly based on your children's interests and energy levels. The most important thing is that everyone enjoys the adventure and comes away with a greater appreciation for the wonders of science!

Engaging Younger Children (Ages 3-7)

While many of the experiences on this Science & Education Trail are fascinating for older children and adults, you might need some strategies to keep younger children engaged. Here are some ideas:

1. **Biomedical Bingo**: Create a simple bingo card with pictures of things they might see at the Barcelona Biomedical Research Park (microscopes, lab coats, test tubes, etc.). Have them mark off items as they spot them during the tour.

1. **Color-Changing Chameleon**: At the Glòries Tower tech hub, give young children a paper chameleon cutout. At each new exhibit or company window, have them color a small part of the chameleon to represent what they've seen, gradually creating a multi-colored memory of their visit.

1. **Park Texture Hunt**: In Ciutadella Park, give young children a sheet with different textures pictured (smooth, rough, bumpy, etc.). Have them find natural objects that match each texture, teaching them to observe their environment closely.

1. **Bubble Science Kit**: Prepare a small bubble-making kit to use in the park. Experiment with different shaped wands and discuss why bubbles are always round, introducing basic concepts of surface tension in a fun way.

Engaging Older Children and Teens (Ages 8-15)

For older children and teenagers, you can dive deeper into scientific concepts and encourage more independent exploration:

1. **Barcelona Science Scavenger Hunt**: Create a more complex scavenger hunt that requires older kids to find specific information at each location. For example, they might need to discover what type of microscope is used in a particular lab at the Biomedical Research Park, or find out how many startups are housed in the Glòries tech hub.

1. **Tech Trend Tracker**: Challenge teens to identify and research emerging technology trends they spot during the visit to the Glòries tech hub. Have them create a brief presentation for the family about how these technologies might impact daily life in the future.

1. **Citizen Science Project**: Introduce older kids to real citizen science projects they can contribute to during your trip. For example, they could use the iNaturalist app to document plant and animal species in Ciutadella Park, contributing to global biodiversity databases.

1. **Science Ethics Debate**: After the visit to the Biomedical Research Park, engage teens in a family discussion about the ethical implications of advanced biomedical research. Topics could include genetic engineering, animal testing, or the privacy concerns of personalized medicine.

1. **DIY Tech Workshop**: Inspired by the Maker Space at Glòries Tower, challenge older children to design and prototype their own invention using simple materials you can carry with you (like cardboard, tape, string, etc.). They can present their invention to the family over dinner.

Local Scientists and Innovators

To add more context to your science adventure, introduce your family to some of Barcelona's notable scientists and innovators. This can help children connect the scientific principles they're learning about to real people and local history:

1. **Ignasi Fina i Comas**: A pioneering figure in public health, Fina worked tirelessly to improve hygiene and combat epidemics in early 20th century Barcelona. His work laid the foundation for many of the biomedical research initiatives you'll learn about at the Barcelona Biomedical Research Park.

1. **Oriol Valls**: This contemporary Catalan physicist has made significant contributions to the field of nanoscience. His work on molecular electronics relates to some of the cutting-edge technology you might see in the Glòries tech hub.

1. **Josefina Castellví i Piulachs**: An oceanographer and biologist, Castellví was the first Spanish scientist to participate in Antarctic research expeditions. Her work in marine microbiology connects to the biodiversity research you'll learn about in Ciutadella Park.

1. **Lluís Torner**: A prominent figure in photonics, Torner founded the Institute of Photonic Sciences in Barcelona. His work on the manipulation of light relates to some of the technology you might encounter in the Glòries area.

1. **Bonaventura Clotet**: A world-renowned HIV researcher based in Barcelona, Clotet's work exemplifies the kind of impactful biomedical research happening in institutions like the one you'll visit.

Extended Learning Opportunities

To make the most of your Science & Education Trail adventure, consider these extended learning opportunities:

1. **Barcelona Supercomputing Center Virtual Tour**: While not part of our physical itinerary, the Barcelona Supercomputing Center offers a fascinating virtual tour. This could be a great evening activity at your accommodation, connecting to the tech themes you've explored during the day.

1. **Tibidabo Amusement Park**: For a fun way to apply physics concepts, consider a visit to Tibidabo Amusement Park on another day. Challenge your children to explain the forces at work on different rides, combining entertainment with practical application of scientific principles.

1. **Beach Ecology Exploration**: Barcelona's beaches offer a different kind of scientific exploration. Consider a guided marine ecology tour to learn about Mediterranean sea life and coastal ecosystems.

1. **CCCB (Centre de Cultura Contemporània de Barcelona)**: This cultural center often hosts exhibitions at the intersection of science, technology, and culture. Check their schedule for any relevant exhibitions during your visit.

1. **Collserola Natural Park**: For families interested in environmental science, consider a guided nature walk in Collserola Natural Park. Learn about local flora and fauna, and discuss concepts of ecology and conservation.

127

Wrapping Up Your Science Adventure

As your Science & Education Trail through Barcelona comes to an end, take some time to reflect on and consolidate your family's learning experiences:

1. **Family Science Symposium**: On your last evening in Barcelona, host a family "science symposium" where each family member presents their favorite discovery or learning from the trip. Younger children can draw pictures, while older ones might prepare short presentations.

1. **Barcelona Science Mystery Box**: Throughout your adventure, collect small mementos (with permission) from each location – perhaps a pebble from Ciutadella Park, a 3D printed object from the Maker Space, or a brochure from the Biomedical Research Park. Place these in a "mystery box" to unpack when you get home, using each object to recall and discuss what you learned.

1. **Future Scientist Vision Board**: Inspire your children to consider careers in science by creating a vision board. Use brochures collected during your trip, printouts of photos you've taken, and drawing materials to visualize potential future careers or scientific achievements they'd like to pursue.

1. **Barcelona Science Quiz Night**: Create a fun, family quiz night using facts learned during your adventure. Award small science-themed prizes (like a small crystal growing kit or a pocket microscope) for correct answers.

1. **Science Pen Pals**: Encourage your children to keep in touch with any young scientists they may have met during workshops or events. This can foster long-term interest in science and provide opportunities for cultural exchange.

G. **Plan a Home Science Lab**: Based on the experiments and demonstrations you've seen, make plans for creating a small science lab space at home. Discuss which simple experiments you could recreate or how you might continue exploring the scientific principles you've encountered in Barcelona.

Practical Information and Tips

To ensure your Science & Education Trail runs smoothly, here are some practical tips:

1. **Reservations**: Many of the activities, especially guided tours and workshops, require advance reservations. Book these as early as possible to secure your spots.

1. **Transportation**: Consider purchasing a multi-day public transportation pass. Barcelona has an excellent public transit system that can easily get you to all the locations on this itinerary.

1. **Weather Preparedness**: Barcelona can get quite hot, especially in summer. Bring refillable water bottles, sunscreen, and hats, particularly for the outdoor activities in Ciutadella Park.

128

1. **Language**: While many scientific terms are similar across languages, it can be helpful to learn a few key scientific words in Catalan or Spanish before your trip.

1. **Snacks**: Pack some brain-boosting snacks like nuts, fruit, or granola bars. Scientific exploration can be hungry work!

G. **Photography Rules**: Check the photography policies at each location. Some research areas may have restrictions on taking photos.

7. **Dress Code**: For the visit to the Biomedical Research Park, closed-toe shoes may be required for safety reasons.

8. **Accessibility**: If anyone in your group has specific accessibility needs, contact the venues in advance to ensure appropriate accommodations.

9. **Local Customs**: Familiarize yourself with local customs and etiquette, especially when interacting with scientists and researchers.

Remember, the goal of the Science & Education Trail is not just to see and do, but to inspire a lifelong love of learning and discovery. By engaging with science in this hands-on, real-world way, you're helping to nurture the next generation of scientists, thinkers, and innovators.

As you leave Barcelona, encourage your family to keep asking questions, staying curious, and looking for the science in everyday life. The adventure doesn't end here – it's just the beginning of a lifelong journey of discovery!

Additional Resources

To further enrich your Barcelona Science & Education experience, here are some additional resources:

1. **Books**:

- "The Barcelona Science Trail" by Maria Ruiz (fictional - a kid-friendly mystery story set in Barcelona's scientific institutions)

- "Catalonia's Contribution to Science" by Xavier Duran (for older readers interested in the region's scientific history)

2. **Websites**:

- Barcelona Science Tourism: (fictional - a site with up-to-date information on science-related events and activities in the city)

- Catalan Association for Science Communication: (real - for those interested in science events and communication in Catalonia)

3. **Apps**:
  - "Barcelona Science Explorer" (fictional - an app with science-themed walking tours of the city)
  - "ScienceNow Barcelona" (fictional - real-time updates on science events and activities happening in the city)

   4. **Local Science Magazines**:
   - "Investigación y Ciencia" (the Spanish edition of Scientific American)
   - "Muy Interesante" (a popular science magazine in Spanish)

   5. **Science Podcasts in Spanish**:
   - "Ciencia al Cubo" by Radio 5 RNE
   - "Coffee Break: Señal y Ruido" by Radio Primavera Sound

These resources can help you prepare for your trip, provide entertainment and learning opportunities during downtime, and allow you to continue your Barcelona science adventure even after you return home.

Hey there, adventure-seeking families! You've already discovered some of Barcelona's most famous attractions, but this magical city has so much more to offer. In this chapter, we're going to uncover some hidden gems and lesser-known spots that will make your family trip even more unforgettable. So, put on your explorer hats and get ready for some extra- special Barcelona adventures!

Magical Gardens and Green Spaces Parc del Laberint d'Horta

Imagine stepping into a real-life maze surrounded by lush greenery and mythological sculptures. That's exactly what you'll find at the Parc del Laberint d'Horta! This enchanting park is Barcelona's oldest garden, dating back to the 18th century.

Fun for the little ones (3-7): The hedge maze is perfect for a game of hide-and-seek. Just make sure to keep an eye on the littlest explorers!

Cool for the older kids (8-15): Challenge them to find the center of the maze, where a statue of Eros, the God of Love, awaits. Time them and see who can do it fastest!

Jardins de Joan Brossa

Tucked away on Montjuïc hill, these gardens offer a unique blend of nature and art. Named after the famous Catalan poet Joan Brossa, the park features quirky sculptures and interactive installations.
- Look out for the giant letters scattered throughout the park – they spell out "Brossaparc"!
- Find the oversize magic hat – a nod to Brossa's love for magic and illusions.

- Enjoy panoramic views of the city from various vantage points.

Family challenge: See who can spot the most unusual sculptures or installations. The winner gets to choose the next ice cream flavor!

Beach Alternatives

While Barcelona's main beaches are fantastic, sometimes it's nice to escape the crowds. Here are a couple of alternatives:

Platja de Garraf

Just a short train ride south of Barcelona, you'll find the charming beach of Garraf. Its colorful beach huts and calm waters make it a perfect spot for a family day out.
What makes it special:

1. Shallow waters, ideal for younger children
2. Iconic white and green beach huts (great for photos!)
3. Less crowded than city beaches
4. Beachside restaurants serving fresh seafood.

Cala Jugadora

For the more adventurous families, consider a day trip to Cala Jugadora in the Cap de Creus Natural Park. This secluded cove offers crystal-clear waters and dramatic rocky landscapes.

Warning: The trek to the beach can be challenging, so it's better suited for families with older children or teens who enjoy hiking.

Tips for visiting:

- Wear sturdy shoes for the walk down to the cove
- Pack plenty of water and snacks
- Bring snorkeling gear to explore the rich marine life

Quirky Museums and Interactive Experiences

Barcelona is home to some world-class museums, but these lesser-known gems offer unique experiences that your kids won't forget!

Museu del Videojoc (Barcelona Arcade)

Step into a time machine and introduce your kids to the video games of your youth! This small but mighty museum showcases the evolution of video games from the 1970s to the present day.

What to expect:

- Playable retro consoles and arcade machines
- Interactive exhibits on game design and technology
- Special events and tournaments (check their schedule!)

Address: Carrer de Sant Pere Més Alt, 4

Museu de la Xocolata

Who doesn't love chocolate? This sweet museum is dedicated to the history and artistry of chocolate-making.

Highlights:

- Learn about the journey of chocolate from bean to bar
- Marvel at intricate chocolate sculptures
- Participate in chocolate-making workshops (book in advance!)

Fun fact: Your entry ticket is a chocolate bar!
Address: Carrer del Comerç, 3G

Museu de les Il·lusions

Prepare to have your mind blown at the Museum of Illusions! This interactive museum is filled with optical illusions, holograms, and mind- bending exhibits that will fascinate visitors of all ages.

Must-see exhibits:

- The Vortex Tunnel (warning: may cause dizziness!)
- The Ames Room, where people appear to grow and shrink
- The Head on a Platter illusion (great for silly family photos)

Address: Carrer del Dr. Aiguader, 17

Hidden Architectural Gems

We all know about Gaudí's masterpieces, but Barcelona has many other architectural wonders waiting to be discovered!

Casa de les Punxes

This fairy-tale-like building, also known as Casa Terradas, was designed by Josep Puig i Cadafalch, a contemporary of Gaudí. Its pointed towers (punxes in Catalan) give it a magical, castle-like appearance.
    Why kids will love it:

    - Audio guide narrated by a dragon (available in multiple languages)
    - Rooftop terrace with great views and a "dragon's cave"
    - Interactive exhibits about Catalan legends and traditions

    Address: Avinguda Diagonal, 420

Casa Vicens

Gaudí's first major project, Casa Vicens, is often overlooked by tourists but is a true hidden gem. Recently opened to the public, this colorful house showcases the early genius of Barcelona's most famous architect.
    Highlights for families:

    - Scavenger hunt activity sheets for kids
    - Beautiful gardens with a fountain
    - Stunning tile work and nature-inspired designs

    Pro tip: Book tickets online in advance to avoid queues.
    Address: Carrer de les Carolines, 20-2G

Outdoor Adventures

Barcelona's surroundings offer plenty of opportunities for outdoor fun and adventure!

Collserola Natural Park

Just a short trip from the city center, Collserola Natural Park is a vast green space perfect for hiking, cycling, and picnicking.
Family-friendly activities:

1. Rent bikes and explore the numerous trails
2. Visit the Collserola Tower for panoramic views
3. Look out for wild boars, rabbits, and various bird species
4. Enjoy a picnic with a view of the city

How to get there: Take the FGC train to Baixador de Vallvidrera station.

Montserrat

While not exactly in Barcelona, the stunning mountain of Montserrat makes for an unforgettable day trip. The uniquely shaped peaks and the famous monastery perched on the mountainside will leave your family in awe.
Things to do:

- Take the cable car or rack railway up the mountain
- Visit the Santa Maria de Montserrat Abbey
- Hike easy trails suitable for children
- Try the local cheese and honey at the market

Local Experiences

Family Paella Cooking Class
Learn to make Spain's most famous dish as a family! Many cooking schools in Barcelona offer family-friendly classes where you can learn to make authentic paella.
What to expect:

- Shop for ingredients at a local market
- Learn about the history and traditions of paella
- Cook (and eat!) your own paella
- Take home the recipe to recreate the magic at home

Recommended schools:

- Barcelona Cooking
- Cook & Taste

Seasonal Events

Depending on when you visit, you might catch one of these fantastic events:

La Mercè Festival (September)

Barcelona's biggest street party! This festival honors the city's patron saint with parades, concerts, and spectacular events.
Don't miss:

- The correfoc (fire run) – watch from a safe distance!
- Giant papier-mâché figures parading through the streets
- Projection mapping shows on prominent buildings
- Castellers (human tower building competitions.

Don't miss:

- The correfoc (fire run) – watch from a safe distance!
- Giant papier-mâché figures parading through the streets
- Projection mapping shows on prominent buildings
- Castellers (human tower building competitions)

Santa Llúcia Christmas Fair (December)

Get into the holiday spirit at this traditional Christmas market held in front of the Barcelona Cathedral.
What to look for:

- Traditional Catalan Christmas decorations
- The caga tió (pooping log) – a quirky Catalan Christmas tradition
- Handmade crafts and local delicacies
- Christmas tree made of recycled materials

Hidden Food Gems

Barcelona is a foodie paradise, but here are some lesser-known spots your family will love:

Gelaaati di Marco

Tucked away in the Gothic Quarter, this artisanal gelato shop offers unique flavors that change daily.
Must-try flavors:

- Crema Catalana (like crème brûlée ice cream!)
- Chocolate con Churros
- Seasonal fruit sorbets

Address: Carrer de la Llibreteria, 7

La Boqueria Cooking

While La Boqueria market is well-known, not many tourists know about the cooking classes held right above the market stalls!
    What makes it special:

   - Shop for ingredients in the historic market
   - Cook traditional Catalan dishes
   - Enjoy your creations with a view of the bustling market below

   Book in advance: Classes fill up quickly, especially during peak season.

Off-the-Beaten-Path Photo Ops

Capture unique family memories at these Instagram-worthy spots:
    1. **The whale skeleton at the Barcelona Zoo** – Even if you don't visit the zoo, you can see this massive skeleton from outside!
    2. **The dragon staircase at Finca Güell** – Less crowded than Park Güell, but equally magical.
    3. **The colorful Horta Labyrinth** – Get lost in the maze and snap some whimsical photos.
    4. **The giant fish sculpture at Port Olímpic** – This golden fish by Frank Gehry is particularly stunning at sunset.

Fun Barcelona Facts for Kids

Impress your little ones with these cool tidbits about Barcelona:
    - Barcelona has a beach that's over 4 km long! That's like 40 football fields put end to end.
    - The Sagrada Familia has been under construction for over 140 years – longer than any other building in the world

- There's a giant mammoth statue in Barcelona. Can you find it? (Hint: It's near the port)

- Barcelona's main street, La Rambla, used to be a river!

- The famous architect Antoni Gaudí was once arrested for refusing to speak Spanish (he only spoke Catalan).

Final Tips for Your Barcelona Adventure

1. **Learn a few Catalan phrases** – The locals will appreciate your effort!
2. **Try the drinking fountains** – Barcelona's tap water is safe and delicious.
3. **Look up** – Some of the city's best architecture is above eye level.
4. **Embrace siesta time** – Many shops close in the afternoon, perfect for a family rest.
5. **Get a T-familiar ticket** – This multi-day, multi-journey ticket is great for families using public transport.

Remember, the best adventures often happen when you least expect them. So while you're ticking off the must-see sights, don't be afraid to wander down that intriguing side street or pop into that quirky-looking shop.

Barcelona is a city full of surprises, waiting for your family to discover them!

¡Que os divirtáis! (Have fun!)

141

CHAPTER NINE - Resources and Additional Information

Welcome to your one-stop shop for all the extra tidbits, helpful links, and insider knowledge you'll need to make your family adventure in Barcelona unforgettable! We've combed through every nook and cranny of this guide to bring you a well-organized treasure trove of information. So, grab a cup of coffee (or a glass of horchata!), and let's dive in!

Essential Websites and Apps

Official Tourism Websites
: The official tourism website for Barcelona. Available in multiple languages.
: The city council's website with information on events, services, and local news.
Must-Have Apps

1. **TMB App**: Real-time public transport information for Barcelona.

2. **Barcelona Official Guide**: Comprehensive city guide with offline maps.
3. **Glovo**: Food delivery app, great for those nights when you're too tired to go out.
4. **Meetup**: Find family-friendly events and meet other traveling families.
Ticketing and Reservations
-: Official city pass for attractions and transport.
- [Tibidabo Amusement Park Book tickets for Barcelona's hilltop amusement park.

- [Park Güell] Reserve your spot at this iconic Gaudí park.

Transportation Tips

Public Transport

- **T-familiar ticket**: Multi-day, multi-journey ticket perfect for families.

- **Metro operating hours**:

- Sunday to Thursday: 5:00 AM - 12:00 AM

- Friday: 5:00 AM - 2:00 AM

143

Biking in Barcelona
- [Biking] Barcelona's bike-sharing system (requires long-term subscription).

- Numerous private bike rental companies available throughout the city.

Taxis and Ride-sharing

- **Cabify**: Popular ride-sharing app in Barcelona.
- **Free Now**: App for hailing official city taxis.

Pro Tip: Always have some cash on hand for smaller establishments and traditional taxis.

Family-Friendly Dining

Kid-Friendly Restaurants

1. **Pudding**: Whimsical café with play areas for children.
2. **Semproniana**: Offers cooking workshops for kids.
3. **La Boqueria Market**: Various stalls with local treats.

Must-Try Local Dishes

- Paella
- Crema Catalana
- Pa amb tomàquet (bread with tomato)
- Bombas (potato croquettes)

Meal Times in Barcelona:

> - Breakfast: 7:00 AM - 9:00 AM
> - Lunch: 2:00 PM - 4:00 PM
> - Dinner: 9:00 PM - 11:00 PM

Seasonal Events and Festivals

Month	Event	Description
April	Sant Jordi	Book and rose festival
June	Sónar	Music and technology festival
August	Festa Major de Gràcia	Neighborhood street festival
September	La Mercè	Barcelona's largest street party
December	Fira de Santa Llúcia	Traditional Christmas market

Rainy Day Activities

1. **CosmoCaixa**: Interactive science museum.
2. **L'Aquàrium**: One of Europe's largest aquariums.
3. **MOCO Museum**: Modern and contemporary art.
4. **Museu de la Xocolata**: Chocolate museum with workshops.
5. **Poble Espanyol**: Indoor-outdoor museum of Spanish architecture.

Outdoor Spaces and Playgrounds

- **Parc de la Ciutadella**: Central park with a lake, zoo, and museums.
- **Parc del Laberint d'Horta**: Historic park with a hedge maze.
- **Parc de Poblenou**: Modern park with unique play structures.
- **Jardins de Joan Brossa**: Quirky park with literary-themed play areas.

Beach Safety and Etiquette

Barcelona Beach Flags:

- Green: Safe to swim
- Yellow: Caution advised
- Red: Dangerous conditions, no swimming

145

Language Basics

While many locals speak English, learning a few Catalan phrases can go a long way:

- "Bon dia" - Good morning
- "Sisplau" - Please
- "Gràcies" - Thank you
- "On és...?" - Where is...?

Emergency Information

- **Emergency number**: 112

- **Tourist police**: +34 932 5G2 777

Accessibility Resources

- [Barcelona Turisme Accessibility Guide]
- Many beaches have accessible facilities and amphibious chairs available.
- Most major attractions and public transport are wheelchair accessible.

Eco-Friendly Barcelona Sustainable Tourism Tips:

1. Use public transport or bike-sharing services.
2. Bring reusable water bottles (tap water is safe to drink).
3. Shop at local markets for souvenirs.
4. Participate in beach clean-up events (check local listings).

Money-Saving Tips

1. **Barcelona Card**: Offers free public transport and discounts on attractions.
2. **Free Museum Days**: Many museums offer free entry on the first Sunday of each month.
3. **Menu del Día**: Fixed-price lunch menus, usually a great value.
4. **Picnic in the Park**: Save on meals by picnicking in Barcelona's beautiful parks.

Final Thoughts

Remember, the best adventures often come from unexpected discoveries. Don't be afraid to wander off the beaten path, chat with locals, and create your own Barcelona story. This city has a way of surprising and delighting visitors of all ages, so keep your eyes open and your sense of wonder alive!

We hope this resource guide helps you navigate the enchanting city of Barcelona with ease and excitement. From all of us at the Mini-Adventure Planner team, we wish you and your family an unforgettable journey filled with laughter, learning, and lots of delicious tapas!

Bon viatge i fins aviat! (Have a good trip and see you soon!)

147

CHAPTER TEN - Wrapping Up This Adventure

As we come to the end of our Mini-Adventure Planner for Barcelona, we hope you're brimming with excitement for the incredible journey that awaits you and your family. But remember, dear adventurers, this guide is just the beginning – a springboard for the countless discoveries you'll make in this enchanting city.

Encouraging Continued Exploration

Barcelona is a city that reveals its secrets slowly, like a masterful magician with an endless supply of tricks up their sleeve. Each corner you turn, each narrow alley you explore, holds the potential for a new adventure, a hidden gem, or a memory that will last a lifetime.

We've shared some of our favorite family-friendly spots and activities, but the true magic of Barcelona lies in the unexpected. That quaint café you stumble upon during an impromptu detour, the street performer who makes your little one giggle uncontrollably, or the breathtaking view you discover while getting "lost" in the winding streets of the Gothic Quarter – these are the moments that will define your Barcelona experience.

So, we encourage you to use this guide as a starting point, but don't be afraid to color outside the lines. Let your curiosity be your compass. If a vibrant mural catches your eye, stop and admire it. If the aroma of freshly baked bread lures you down an unfamiliar street, follow your nose. If your children are fascinated by a peculiar statue or fountain, take the time to make up stories about its origin.

Remember, the best family adventures are often unscripted. Embrace the spontaneity that travel offers, and allow Barcelona to surprise and delight you at every turn. After all, it's not just about checking off items on a to-do list; it's about creating a tapestry of experiences that your family will cherish for years to come.

Staying Connected and Sharing Experiences

Your Barcelona adventure doesn't have to end when you board your flight home. In fact, we believe that sharing your experiences and staying connected with fellow travelers can extend the joy of your trip long after you've unpacked your suitcases.

We'd love to hear about your family's Barcelona adventures! Did you discover a family-friendly restaurant that we missed? Did your kids fall in love with a playground we didn't mention? Or perhaps you have a funny story about getting lost in the Labyrinth Park of Horta? Your experiences and insights are invaluable and can help other families make the most of their Barcelona adventures.

Here are some ways you can share your experiences and stay connected:

1. **Use our official hashtag**: When posting your Barcelona family photos on social media, use the hashtag #MiniBcnAdventures. This allows other families to find your posts and get inspired by your experiences.

1. **Join our Facebook group**: We've created a Facebook group called "Mini-Adventure Planners: Barcelona Edition" where you can connect with other families, share tips, and even arrange meetups if your trips overlap.

1. **Write a blog post**: If you're feeling particularly inspired, why not write a blog post about your family's Barcelona adventure? We'd be thrilled to feature some of the best stories on our website.

1. **Send us an email**: We love receiving personal stories and photos. Send your Barcelona tales to stories@miniadventureplanner.com, and you might see them featured in the next edition of our guide!

The Adventure Continues

As we close this chapter of your Mini-Adventure Planner, we want to remind you that the real adventure is just beginning. Barcelona is not just a destination; it's an experience, a feeling, a state of mind. It's the excitement of trying new foods, the wonder of walking in the footsteps of great artists and architects, and the joy of watching your children's eyes light up as they soak in the vibrant culture around them.

Take a moment to imagine your family strolling down Las Ramblas, the sun warming your faces as street performers entertain the crowds. Picture the look of awe on your children's faces as they gaze up at the intricate spires of the Sagrada Família. Envision the laughter and splashes as you play together on the shores of Barceloneta Beach.

From all of us at the Mini-Adventure Planner team, we wish you safe travels, incredible discoveries, and memories that will last a lifetime. May your family adventure in Barcelona be everything you've dreamed of and more.

Bon viatge, exploradors petits i grans! (Have a great trip, explorers big and small!)

And remember, in the words of the great Catalan architect Antoni Gaudí, "To do things right, first you need love, then technique." So go forth with love in your hearts, adventure in your souls, and this guide in your hands. Barcelona awaits!

151

About the Author

Hi, I'm Christopher Neil, author and avid travel enthusiast and the creator of the Mini-Adventure Planner series. I've embrassed my love for travel to bring you these family-friendly travel guides.

I quickly realized that while there were plenty of travel guides out there, few catered to the unique needs and interests of families with young children.

And so, armed with a backpack full of snacks, a camera, and an insatiable curiosity, I set out to change that!

Over the years, I've had the joy of traipsing through cobblestone streets, people watching from street cafe's and taste-testing ice cream flavors (it's a tough job, but someone's got to do it!) in cities across the globe. Barcelona, with its vibrant colors, whimsical architecture, and child-friendly atmosphere, holds a special place in my heart – and I'm thrilled to share its magic with you through this guide.

When I'm not travelling, I'm probably planning our next family adventure, or answering emails from fellow travelers.

My goal with the Mini-Adventure Planner series is simple: to help families create unforgettable memories together, one city at a time. I believe that travel is one of the greatest gifts we can give our children – it opens their minds, sparks their curiosity, and teaches them about the beautiful diversity of our world.

I hope this guide helps you navigate the enchanting city of Barcelona with ease, excitement, and a spirit of discovery. Remember, the best family adventures are the ones where you expect the unexpected and embrace the joyful chaos that comes with traveling with kids!

Happy travels, and may your family adventures be filled with laughter, learning, and lots of delicious local treats!

Bon voyage! Christopher

153

Thank you for making it this far!

I greatly appreciate the time you took to give my book a read,as a small indie publisher it means a lot and I hope that I am making a difference for you visit to Barcelona.

If you have G0 seconds your honest feedback on Amazon would mean the world to me., it does wonders for the book and I love hearing about your experience with it.

To Leave Your Feedback

1. Open your camera App
2. Point your mobile device at the QR code below
3. The review page will appear in your web browser

Or

You can click this link: https://www.amazon.com/dp/[1]
B0DK2LV8GX

---

1. http://www.amazon.com/dp/

About the Author

The wonder of Barcelona - Stroll down Las Ramblas, visit the beaches and be amazed by the beauty of the architecture of Gaudi's buildings. In the guide by serial traveller Christopher Neil you will find all that you need for a comprehensive visit to this fabulous city.

Plan your adventure to suit you and your family, explore and discover the culture and sights.

See the arts and take the science and Education Trail, that your children will love.

For the foodie family enjoy snack in the cosy street bars or meals in some of Barcelona's best restaurants. You will find some of the best Tapas down the side streets as well as other hidden gems that you might not have expected

Additional recommendations for a visit not normally found in the standard city guides as well as all details and location of: Las Ramblas, Barri Gòtic, El Born, Eixample, Montjuïc, and more.

Resources such as the official tourism website, essential Apps to accompany your visit, transport tips including the Hop-on Hop-off Bus which is a must. Seasonal events and festivals, rainy day activities, outdoor spaces and parks, language basics, eco-friendly sustainable tips, money saving tips and more.

If your visit to Barcelona is for just a day or a few days try Christopher Neil's Pocket Itinery (coming soon)

Make the most of your Barcelona family adventure.